SPOOKY
Pennsylvania

SPOOKY
Pennsylvania

*Tales of Hauntings, Strange Happenings,
and Other Local Lore*

RETOLD BY S. E. SCHLOSSER

ILLUSTRATED BY PAUL G. HOFFMAN

INSIDERS' GUIDE®

GUILFORD, CONNECTICUT
AN IMPRINT OF THE GLOBE PEQUOT PRESS

INSIDERS' GUIDE®

Copyright © 2007 by S. E. Schlosser

Text design by Lisa Reneson
Illustrations and map border by Paul G. Hoffman
Map by Lisa Reneson © Morris Book Publishing, LLC

Library of Congress Cataloging-in-Publication Data is available.

ISBN-13: 978-0-7627-3996-7
ISBN-10: 0-7627-3996-7

Manufactured in the United States of America
First Edition/Second Printing

For my grandmother, Mildred Schlosser, who shared with me her Pennsylvania Dutch heritage. And for my family—David, Dena, Tim, Arlene, Hannah, Emma, Nathan, Ben, Deb, Gabe, Clare, Jack, and Karen.

For Tony and Joyce Torlish, and for Anne Bisco, who have kindly taken me into their home and their hearts on more than one occasion. With my thanks!

For Jerry, Liz, Len, Shannon, and Lydia, who have the pleasure and privilege of living in Pennsylvania.

For Cookie, Dave, Millie, Nathan, Laura, and Virginia. Thank you for your hospitality and the wonderful stories.

And for Mimi Egan, who grew up in the 'Burgh and who still remembers its stories with fondness.

* * *

Contents

Contents

Contents

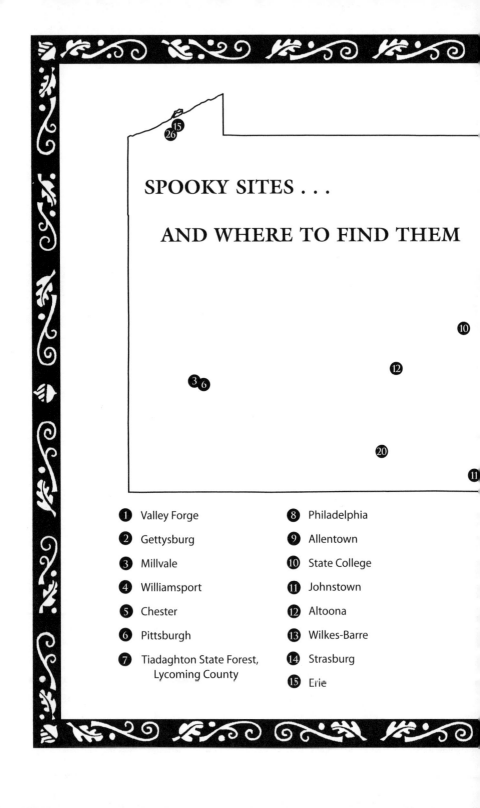

SPOOKY SITES . . .

AND WHERE TO FIND THEM

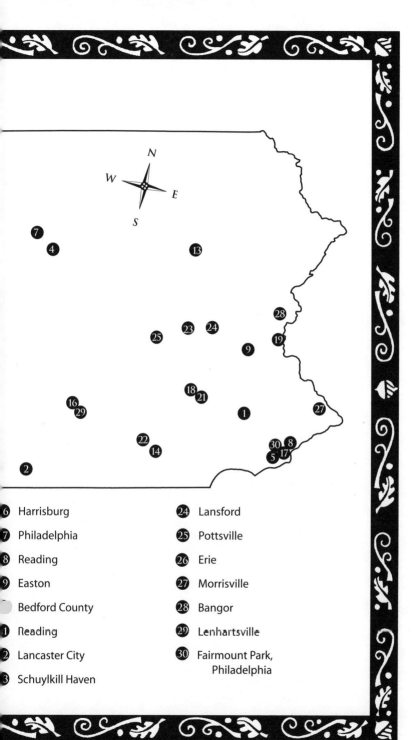

Contents

Introduction

My twice-great grandfather, Richard Johnson, was a Pennsylvania Dutch "powwow doctor" living in Bangor ("Wild-fire"). As a powwow doctor, he practiced natural medicine, sometimes combined with magic. Old Man Johnson was a faith healer, credited with the miraculous curing of broken bones and illness of all kinds by the folks of Bangor, though he would never take a patient who had cancer for fear it would "turn back on him." But he was also, sad to say, a hex doctor who could curse people and cause bad things to happen to them.

The only physician in a poor, small-town community, Richard Johnson was much in demand, but he did not have enough work to make a living of it. And although there were a few skeptics among them who did not believe in "hoodoo," the surrounding community held him in some awe.

My paternal grandmother once spent a summer with Old Man Johnson, learning the ways of the faith healer. She later studied to be a nurse and did quite a bit of healing in her time, though I believe she stuck to standard medical practice.

When I was growing up, my grandmother's house was only a few houses up the block from mine. From the moment I learned to walk, I would toddle up the road to see my Pennsylvania Dutch Grandma, a fact that nearly drove my mother to an early grave. Grandma's house was filled with hex signs (of the friendly sort) and Pennsylvania Dutch folk sayings. As a young child, I remember puzzling over a plaque that read THROW THE COW OVER THE FENCE SOME HAY and depicted a farmer tossing a placid bovine over a picket fence.

Grandma also cooked the traditional Pennsylvania Dutch meals, including dandelion greens, which I refused to eat, and sausage and sauerkraut, which is still one of my favorite meals. She would make homemade bread and shoofly pie and all sorts of other mouthwatering recipes that were passed down from her mother's mother. Sometimes, she spoke in the German dialect that was common among the Pennsylvania Dutch living in Allentown and the surrounding regions.

Although a member of the church, with a strong personal faith, my grandmother still retained many of her Pennsylvania Dutch cultural traditions—such as the belief in hexes—until the day she died. She left me with a rich heritage full of folklore and funny sayings and wonderful food that has done much to enhance my life over the years. I miss her still.

Having such a close family tie to Pennsylvania made me approach the collection of spooky folktales from this wonderful state with delight. I stayed the weekend with a cousin in Allentown and discovered that I was sleeping in a haunted house ("The Toy Room"). I paid a visit to Lancaster County and found myself in a cemetery where a certain woman's statue likes to take a stroll on the anniversary of her death ("The Walking Statue"). In Strasburg, I window-shopped on Main Street, where it is said that a phantom coach will drive right before a thunderstorm. (Alas, the day was clear, and no ghosts appeared during my walk.)

Farther afield, there are the ghost of Old Coaly, a mule who sometimes visits with the students at Penn State, and the White Lady, who has been seen hitching a ride to the top of Wopsononock Mountain in Altoona, searching for her dead husband. In Pittsburgh, a steelworker encounters the grisly spirit of an accident victim, and an artist finds himself face-to-face with the ghost of a priest.

Eastern Pennsylvania has several stories that have haunted me long after I penned them. In Philadelphia, the miserable spirit of Edgar Allan Poe still wanders through Fairmount Park ("Nevermore"), while in Wilkes-Barre, the corpse of a miner-minstrel pays a final visit to a dear friend. In Bedford County, a vampire called Morning Star returns to claim the life of an old Native American warrior.

The story that I found the most riveting was the tale of George Washington's ghost, who appeared at a critical moment during the Battle of Gettysburg to help and inspire the Union troops ("George Washington Leads the Way"). It is one of the lesser known ghost stories from that particular battle, but to me, it is one of the best.

From the Axe Murder Hollow in Erie to the country's first public library in Philadelphia, Pennsylvania is filled with spooky tales and an incredibly rich folklore that makes it unique. I've loved every moment of my journey in this wonderful state, and I am very proud of my Pennsylvania Dutch heritage.

Auf Weidersehn,
Sandy Schlosser

PART ONE
Ghost Stories

The Phantom Drummer

VALLEY FORGE

When Colonel Howell of the British Army chanced to meet the daughter of the wealthy farmer Jarrett, who owned land near Valley Forge, he fell head over heels in love. Howell had a bit of a reputation as a womanizer, but it faded away after he met Ruth. The girl had a brother serving under George Washington, and none of her family liked the Redcoats, but so overwhelming was Howell's love for Ruth that it conquered the reluctant maiden's heart.

Ruth and her British soldier met in a secret place near the wall of her garden, which was hidden by a small grove of trees. On the night that Howell proposed, they were embracing in their private corner when the sharp, merry sound of a drummer rang through the garden. At first they ignored the noise, caught up in their plans for the future, but as the sound of the drum grew nearer, Howell started looking about nervously. Leaving Ruth's side, he went to peer over the wall, trying to see the drummer.

Ruth was puzzled by Howell's reaction. No one could see them in this little grove, which was why they used it for their trysts. She found it rather annoying that her newly

THE PHANTOM DRUMMER

betrothed would leave her side at such a moment just to look for a casual drummer practicing in the fields. She changed her attitude, though, when Howell turned from the wall, for he was deathly pale.

"What is wrong?" she cried, hurrying to him.

"There is no one there," Howell told Ruth hoarsely.

Ruth stared at him, frightened by his words. The roll of the drum still rang through the fields beyond the wall.

"But surely. . ." she began. She was interrupted by a phantom rat-a-tat-tat. The sound drew closer. As they listened in horror, it came right through the garden gate just beyond the trees. The invisible drummer entered their little hollow and passed through the wall next to them. Only when the sound ceased altogether did Howell snap out of the fear-induced trance he was in. He convulsively clasped Ruth to his chest. No less frightened, Ruth begged Howell to tell her what it could mean.

"For the last three generations," Howell said shakily, "a phantom drummer has appeared to warn my family of a change in fortunes, some for good, most for ill." Seeing the look on Ruth's face, he tried to shake off his terror. He spoke a few words of reassurance to her, which neither of them believed, kissed her goodbye, and galloped away.

In a skirmish the next day, Colonel Howell was shot. He was brought to Farmer Jarrett's house for nursing, though Ruth's father was reluctant to have a British soldier under his roof. To Ruth's relief, the wound was fairly minor and would soon heal. To add to her joy, her father grew fond of the young man and consented to their marriage if Howell would leave the British army. The colonel made this promise willingly, and a secret marriage was soon arranged.

Then tragedy struck. Orders arrived demanding that Howell rejoin his regiment on the eve of an impending battle. Howell knew that to honorably resign his commission would take months, and he would be forced to fight and kill the Americans in the battle the next day. So he decided to marry Ruth, desert the British army, and hide himself away until it was safe to rejoin the Jarrett household.

Divesting himself of his British uniform, he donned the clothes of a civilian and stood with Ruth before a minister in the parlor of the Jarrett house. As he slipped the wedding ring on his beloved's finger and bent to kiss her, the roll of a drum sounded from outside. Howell and Ruth turned fearfully and listened as the invisible drummer climbed the steps, walked through the room, and exited via the far wall.

Ruth clung to her new husband in terror, while the guests and clergy murmured in awe. Then they heard rough voices outside, and someone pounded on the front door. Suddenly the house was full of British soldiers, come to capture Howell based on the testimony of one of the Jarrett servants, who hated the Redcoats and had betrayed them. Howell was arrested, tried, and shot for desertion. At the moment he died, Ruth, sobbing alone in her bedchamber at home, heard the faint, unmistakable roll of a phantom drum.

George Washington Leads the Way

GETTYSBURG

The lieutenant was at heart a simple man. The only thing he had ever desired was a life of peace in which to marry, work hard for a living, and raise his children. But the war with the South had swept over them all, and so he had become a soldier assigned to the Twentieth Maine, hoping to buy peace for his beloved home with his own life, if necessary.

The lieutenant had never expected such a fierce battle to erupt in a quiet town like Gettysburg, Pennsylvania. However, the Confederate soldiers, tired, hungry, and in need of supplies, had descended upon Gettysburg on July 1, 1863, and the Union soldiers had engaged them in a conflict that soon escalated into a bloodbath. All day it raged as reinforcements arrived from both sides. By the morning of July 2, General Robert E. Lee's entire Army of Northern Virginia with its 75,000 men was arrayed just south of Gettysburg, facing down the 97,000-man Army of the Potomac under the command of General George G. Meade.

The lieutenant felt his whole body trembling as the day wore on; he was not sure if it was with nerves or excitement or both. The Twentieth Maine, under the command of Colonel Joshua Chamberlain, had quickly found themselves defending Little Round Top from the Confederate Army, which was fighting to take the strategically placed hill. They stood with the Fifth Corps of the Union army, staunchly fighting back wave after wave of Confederate soldiers.

The lieutenant sometimes wondered if there would ever be an end to the rifle fire, to the endless waves of enemy soldiers. But their orders were clear: "You are to hold this ground at any cost." And so they held the ground, protecting the Army of the Potomac's left flank.

They were constantly harassed by the Fifteenth Alabama, who kept charging up the hill, testing their weaknesses, trying to outflank them. Their powder was running low, their ammunition dwindling, their strength almost spent. Soldiers ransacked the bodies of the wounded and dead strewn on the hillside, searching for spare cartridge boxes, but even this desperate action did not provide them with enough ammunition to continue their holding action for much longer.

At times, the lieutenant saw more of the enemy than his own men; gaps in the line opened, swallowed, and closed again with sharp, convulsive energy. As they thrust the Fifteenth Alabama back down the hill once again, the lieutenant knew that their next stand would be their last.

In the brief lull that followed, Colonel Chamberlain called his officers to a quick meeting. Five minutes more of such a defensive would finish them, he told them bluntly. As desperate as the chances were, their only hope lay in taking the offense. He then proposed that the Twentieth Maine make a charge against the

Confederates. The lieutenant felt his heart pound at the idea. It was madness, but he could see that the colonel was determined. No one would be able to talk him out of the idea, he knew that from experience, so he stayed silent.

Colonel Chamberlain stepped to the colors, and all the men turned toward him. Then, over the roar of the cannons and the constant gunfire, the colonel shouted: "Fix bayonets!" The men realized at once that their commander was going to order the Twentieth Maine out from behind their covered positions and into a charge against the Confederate army. A murmur of doubt swept through them. They were ordered to hold the hill at any cost, but this . . . this was suicide. Then a few hearty souls shouted the order, and it was passed down the line.

The lieutenant drew a shaky breath and whispered a prayer. Then his eye was caught by a movement farther down the slope. A figure sprang up out of nowhere, right before the enemy line. The lieutenant blinked in shock, recognizing the waistcoat, breeches, jacket, and boots of a Revolutionary War commander. And the face . . . the face was that of General George Washington himself! The semitransparent figure drew his sword and brandished it in the faces of the Confederate soldiers.

The lieutenant felt sudden tears come to his eyes as he stared at the spirit of George Washington defying the Southern soldiers in their bid to split the nation the general and his fellow patriots had fought to create. When the command came to charge, the lieutenant leaped without hesitation from his sheltered spot and ran down the southern slope of Little Round Top toward the ghost of George Washington and the soldiers of the Fifteenth Alabama.

GEORGE WASHINGTON LEADS THE WAY

The lieutenant was vaguely aware that he was alone for a moment as, behind him, the men of the Twentieth Maine hesitated in fear and indecision. Then his fellow soldiers charged, shouting their defiance. Led by Colonel Chamberlain, they raced down the slope. The lieutenant heard one or two of them shout General Washington's name and knew that he was not the only one who had seen the ghost.

The Fifteenth Alabama was caught completely off guard by the suicidal charge. They fought hand to hand for a few moments with the Twentieth Maine, then broke off and retreated. The Union soldiers cheered excitedly, knowing that they had just saved the left flank of the Northern army.

By the end of the three-day battle, the slopes of Little Round Top were covered with the bodies of the dead, as were the Devil's Den and all the areas surrounding them. Historians would later call the Battle of Gettysburg a hallmark victory for the Union, the turning point in the war. It was also the bloodiest single battle of the war, resulting in more than 51,000 soldiers killed, wounded, captured, or missing.

The lieutenant was not sure why his life had been spared, but as he gazed down upon the carnage, he knew that he was one of the lucky ones. And in his heart, he suddenly believed that they would win this war. If the spirit of George Washington himself was willing to lead the way, how could the Northern army fail?

3

The Artist and the Ghost

MILLVALE

Maxo Vanka was commissioned to paint a series of murals for St. Nicholas Croatian Roman Catholic Church in Millvale, on the outskirts of Pittsburgh, during the spring and early summer of 1937. He was Croatian himself, and an artist of great talent and sensitivity. Upon arriving in Millvale, Vanka gave strict instructions to Father Zagar and to the congregation: He was not to be disturbed while he worked. Traffic inside the church after the last Mass finished at 9:00 P.M. was to be limited or nonexistent. To these conditions the good father agreed.

Vanka worked late at night in the relative silence of the church. Outside, he could hear traffic, trains, and the barking of the two parish dogs as they went about their guard duties. Inside was the soft creak, creak, creaking of the scaffolding erected around the walls where he stood to do his work. When he finished painting in the wee hours of the morning, Vanka went over to the parish house, where Father Zagar waited for him with coffee and cake, a gesture of kindness that the artist much appreciated.

One evening, Vanka heard the dogs begin to bark and fuss outside in a rather more fervent way than usual. A moment

11

later, he glanced down through the scaffolding above the altar and saw a priest in black gesturing and praying in the brilliant light he kept beside him to illuminate his work. It was Father Zagar, he assumed, going about his duties in silence so as not to distract him. Vanka appreciated the priest's silence, though for some reason he felt chills deep inside his body at the sight of the dark figure. When he finished his work for the night, he was met by two very anxious dogs that fawned on him as he walked to the rectory to meet Father Zagar for coffee and cake. Vanka asked the priest if he had stopped by that evening to pray, but Father Zagar said he had not done so. The artist thought it strange that the priest should deny being in the sanctuary but held his peace.

Several evenings passed in silence. Then one night, Vanka felt again a strange chill that shuddered through his body, just before he peered down at the altar and saw the gesturing priest in black. He returned to his work on the mural of the Holy Virgin, trying to ignore the figure below. A while later, he saw the dark priest pacing up and down the aisles, muttering to himself in prayer. Suddenly, all the lights in the church were extinguished, save for the one on the scaffold with the artist.

Vanka was frightened and annoyed by the inconvenience. Why had Father Zagar turned off the lights when he knew the artist was working? Breaking off early, he went to the rectory, where he found the priest fast asleep. Ah ha, he thought; Father Zagar must have been sleepwalking. But it was not so.

Hesitantly, Father Zagar told Vanka that a ghostly priest was rumored to haunt St. Nicholas. The members of the parish refused to enter the building late at night out of fear and respect

THE ARTIST AND THE GHOST

for the apparition. Father Zagar confessed that he often stood outside the sanctuary door and watched over the artist during the long evenings while he painted, afraid lest Vanka see the ghost and fall from the scaffolding.

Vanka was rather skeptical about the story of a ghost. Then he remembered the terrible chill that shook his body when he saw the figure in black. Reluctantly, he agreed to allow Father Zagar to keep him company while he painted in the church.

The next night, the two men laughed and talked as Vanka worked on the lovely murals that were taking shape on the walls around them. As a joke, Father Zagar rose, threw his arms wide, and bade the spirit of the dead priest to appear before them. His words were met with a sudden, uncanny stillness. The whole world seemed to hold its breath, and the paintbrush in Vanka's right hand began to shake as a familiar deep chill shuddered through his body.

Then the knocking began. Bang. Bang. Bang. The doors seemed to reverberate under the ghostly hand of the dead priest. Outside, the parish dogs began barking frantically. Father Zagar, his voice shaking, commanded the spirit to depart in peace. The artist's shout cut across his words. Vanka could see the shadowy figure sitting in a pew just behind Father Zagar, gazing upward toward the scaffolding where Vanka stood, paintbrush in hand. The ghost's face was dark and wrinkled and tinged with an unhealthy blue. His eyes, staring up toward the artist, were unseeing, though they seemed to pierce through Vanka's very soul. The ghost leaned against the pew in front of him, his face a picture of abject misery. Vanka began to tremble with a deep fear that had more to do with instinct than mind.

Father Zagar whirled around, searching the pews for a sight of the spirit, but it disappeared when he turned. Privately, Father Zagar was skeptical about the ghost sighting. He concluded that Vanka had imagined the apparition, although he had no explanation for the knocking sound.

But when Father Zagar went to bed later that night, his sleep was troubled by an unseen presence that knocked and clicked and filled the room with an unearthly chill that shuddered through his body. After that, the priest firmly believed in the presence of the ghost, and he prayed that the dead spirit would leave them in peace.

For a few days, Father Zagar's prayers kept the ghost at bay. Confident that the spirit was gone, Father Zagar decided it was safe to relate the dead man's story to Vanka as the artist perched upon the scaffolding, painting industriously through the night. It seemed that a former priest of the parish was rather unscrupulous in nature and had begun neglecting his holy duties to the people. After a few years, the congregation began suspecting that the corrupt man was also pilfering money from the parish, although no formal accusation was made against him. When the priest died, the members of the parish believed that his spirit was forced to remain in the church to do penance for his evil deeds in life. It was believed that the dead priest was attempting to perform the holy acts he should have done in life, and in so doing to finally free his spirit from this earth.

The night after this story was told, the knocking began again. From his perch on the scaffolding, Vanka saw the ghostly figure walk up the main aisle of the sanctuary. Hoarsely, he described the ghost's movements to Father Zagar, who saw nothing. At the front of the sanctuary, on the main altar, stood the light of the eternal flame, which had burned unabated for eight years and was protected from all drafts by the glass surrounding it. As Vanka watched, the ghost walked up to the altar, bent down, and blew it out. Father Zagar gasped in alarm when the eternal light went out, though he still did not see the apparition. Then all the lights in the church went out.

Vanka gave a strangled yell of fear. Half-climbing and half-falling, he managed to descend the ladder beside the scaffolding. His hands shaking too much to paint and his mind filled with a nameless dread, Vanka managed to collect the frozen form of Father Zagar and hustled him out of the sanctuary.

After that, Vanka had to force himself back into the church night after night, and he insisted that Father Zagar join him each evening, since he was afraid to paint alone in that haunted place. Whenever the artist felt the slightest chill, he would leave the church immediately, fearing another encounter with the ghost of the priest, who obviously did not want anyone interfering with his holy duties.

Vanka finished his commission as rapidly as was possible under the strained circumstances. Within two months, he put the finishing touches on the magnificent murals of St. Nicholas and was not slow in leaving the haunted sanctuary to its parishioners and its ghost.

To this day, the lovely murals painted by Maxo Vanka may be seen in St. Nicholas Church in Millvale, on the northern outskirts of Pittsburgh. The spirit of the dead priest has made no recent appearances, although sometimes the parish dogs still bark apprehensively in the night, and a deep, deep chill can be felt in the air.

4

Sweet Cecily's Song

Powderhorn and his family lived on a wide stream near Williamsport. They were a remnant of the Mingo tribe who had remained behind when their people were driven west into the Indian Territory, refusing to leave the land. Their home was located directly across the stream from a Scottish farmer named Ezra McGrady, who treated his Mingo neighbors with respect.

Powderhorn had a young daughter named Sweet Cecily, after the delicate plant used throughout the area for healing. The girl was beautiful and sweet and kind, and all of the men and women in the region were deeply attached to the child, who had the voice of an angel. Sweet Cecily would often climb to a large rock overlooking the stream and sing for hours. The sound of her lovely voice would float in the air for miles, enchanting her neighbors and the raftsmen who worked the stream when it was filled to overflowing during the springtime floods.

As Sweet Cecily grew to womanhood, she fell in love with Wild William, a Mingo man who worked for Farmer

17

McGrady. Wild William would listen to his sweetheart singing as she waited for him atop the rock overlooking the stream and would join her as soon as he finished his tasks for the day. The young couple would sit and talk for hours on their lofty perch. The raftsmen floating down the stream would watch for them and wave as they drifted past the rock. Sometimes Sweet Cecily would sing for them as they navigated the rough waters with their poles.

But a day came when a stranger rode his raft down the stream, a man who did not care for the native families in the area and wished them driven out. When he heard the sweet voice of the Mingo maiden singing an old ballad of her people, he gazed upon her with loathing—and with lust. Docking his raft on the shore, he ran rapidly up the slope toward the rock where she sat waiting for her beloved Wild William to come to her at the end of his day's labors.

Across the stream, Wild William looked up from his work and saw the man approaching Sweet Cecily with such a look of evil intent upon his face that the frantic Mingo lad dropped everything and ran to the stream. As he rowed desperately across the raging water, he saw the man making advances toward the beautiful maiden, who rejected his foul suggestions. In a fury, the man grabbed her by the throat. Wild William leaped ashore and raced up the slope, but by the time he reached the rock at the top, Sweet Cecily lay dead upon the ground, and her murderer had fled the scene and disappeared. William collapsed at his love's side, overcome by horror and grief.

Everyone in the neighborhood was devastated by the lovely girl's tragic death. But the local authorities, when

SWEET CECILY'S SONG

appealed to, did nothing to track down the girl's murderer. In disgust at the white man's treatment of himself and his family, Powderhorn packed everything he owned and left Pennsylvania forever, followed shortly by a disconsolate Wild William, who mourned his lost love his whole life long. The neighbors and raftsmen who had so many times listened in wonder to the lovely song of Sweet Cecily mourned for many months, and spoke bitterly about the fatal spring day when a murderer had stolen her life from them all.

It was early in the spring of the next year that McGrady and his farmhands heard the voice of Sweet Cecily floating out over the ridge from the rock opposite his property. She was singing the same ballad she had sung on the day she was murdered. McGrady dropped everything—as Wild William once had done—and rowed across the stream, his heart pounding with hope. Perhaps Sweet Cecily was not dead! But the rock, when he reached it, was empty. He stood listening with trembling heart as the phantom voice finished its song and then made his way back home. The voice was heard no more that day.

Again and again that spring, the voice of Sweet Cecily rang out over the raging floodwaters of the stream. Several raftsmen were so enchanted by the siren sound that they forgot to pay attention to the stream and overturned their crafts, and the number of deaths on that stretch of stream rose dramatically. Others drew their rafts up on the bank near Farmer McGrady's house and went inside to inquire about the beautiful voice they heard singing on the ledge.

One day, a cruel-faced man came to the farmer's house and demanded to know what had become of the Mingo family who lived across the stream. He was drunk and belligerent, and his anger had been roused by the phantom voice that he had heard singing from the ledge. He seemed to think it a foul trick played on him by the native family. His suspicion and guilt made McGrady suspicious. The farmer drew out the man, learning his name and occupation and other details. McGrady was sure he was looking at the face of Sweet Cecily's murderer.

After the man left, McGrady sent out word to the local residents, identifying the cruel-faced man as Sweet Cecily's murderer. The raftsmen in particular were furious, and they decided to seek vengeance for the lovely girl's death.

The cruel-faced man was spotted on the stream early the next spring, gazing in fear and loathing at the place where Sweet Cecily had once sung her ballads. Recognizing the man as the wanted murderer, a young rafter who was cruising the same stretch of stream aimed his craft at the unsuspecting man's vessel and crashed into it, pitching the murderer into the raging stream. The man was instantly swept away by the fierce waters, his body crushed again and again against the large rocks until he drowned.

The mangled body was picked up farther downstream, and a group of raftsmen buried the murderer unceremoniously in a hole they dug near Powderhorn's abandoned house. As the last of the dirt was flung back on the grave, the beautiful voice of Sweet Cecily rang out from the ledge overlooking the stream. She was singing the old native ballad she had sung on the day she died. The raftsmen stood silent and still until the Mingo maiden had completed her song. On the far side of the stream, Farmer McGrady stood with his hat in his hands and tears in his eyes. Her voice had never sounded so clear and sweet as it did at that moment.

That was the very last time anyone ever heard Sweet Cecily's song.

5

The Last Dance

CHESTER

Quidd sat at a table near the bar, discussing the haunted house on his property with a few of his close friends. The decrepit mansion on his land was once the home of Peter Printz, the governor-general of the Swedish king's American colonies. It had been a grand home, and the governor had entertained many dignitaries there, throwing elegant parties and dinners. But that was long in the past, and the mansion was now practically a ruin and was reputed to house the spirits of the dead.

After eavesdropping on the conversation for a few minutes, Fiddler Matthews put down his instrument and took his glass to the bar for a refill. Leaning against the counter as he waited for his drink, the slender, dark-haired Matthews turned to the man standing beside him and remarked, "Quidd's afraid to sleep on his own property. What a coward!"

The man shifted uneasily and glanced over his shoulder. Belatedly, Matthews became aware that the tavern had fallen silent. He turned and found himself face-to-face with Quidd, who had followed the fiddler to the bar to refresh his own drink. Matthews ducked his head and hunched his shoulders apologetically, but Quidd's posture did not relax.

"Fiddler Matthews, I have a proposition for thee," he said in a booming voice that could be heard in every corner of the tavern. Everyone was watching the encounter between the two men with avid interest. The tall property-owner loomed over the tiny fiddler like a figure of doom.

"What proposition is that?" asked Matthews, turning his palms up in a placating gesture that he hoped would appease Quidd.

"I will give thee five dollars a week if thou will be the caretaker of Printz Hall," said Quidd with a grim, challenging smile.

Matthews swallowed and folded his arms tightly against his chest in an effort to keep his heart from banging through his chest. He didn't mind laughing at ghosts in the warm light of the tavern with his body full of whiskey and many friendly faces in the room. But the idea of staying in the deserted old house with its strange lights and eerie voices that moaned in the dead of night terrified him.

The eyes of everyone in the tavern were upon him, and he knew that to refuse Quidd's request would brand him a coward for the rest of his days. Not to mention that some of Quidd's friends were capable of pummeling him within an inch of his life for daring to mock their companion.

Swallowing hard, Matthews agreed to take the job.

"Good," Quidd said. "Thou may begin tomorrow night."

Quidd accepted his refilled drink from the bartender and returned to his table. Each of his friends gave Matthews a meaningful stare before turning their backs to him. Their looks clearly told the fiddler that he'd better show up at Printz Hall the next evening, or he would feel the results for many months to come.

Matthews took his whiskey and went back to his fiddle, but his songs had lost their edge, and he swiftly wrapped up his playing for the night and went home. "Me and my big mouth," he moaned softly to himself as he trotted home, clutching the fiddle protectively to his chest.

Twilight of the next evening found Matthews installed in the dusty, ruined old house with a slender mattress, a few rough blankets, a stack of wood for the fireplace, his fiddle, and a bottle of "medicinal" whiskey. The trees outside shook and murmured in the rising wind. The bushes and tall grass in the once-immaculate gardens bent under the gale as a storm approached, quickly turning dusk into night.

Matthews lit a fire, stuffed some rags into the broken window panes to keep out the chill, bolted the door, and ate his dinner, his heart thumping painfully in his chest all the while. He took a few gulps of whiskey, which calmed him down, then got out his fiddle. Tuning the strings, he began playing all his favorite songs as the wind whistled and moaned outside and the rain lashed against the windows. But his fingers fumbled on the strings whenever a tree branch knocked against the house or a floorboard creaked, and finally he gave up and went to bed.

Matthews did not know what it was that woke him. Suddenly, his eyes were wide open, and he stared up at the dark ceiling, listening with every fiber of his being. Something was amiss, somewhere. He knew it, although what sound had alerted him, among the howling wind and grinding shutters and lashing rain, he did not know. Then he heard it again: footsteps on the stairs, the tap of a sword as it brushed against the railing. Someone was coming.

The fiddler sat up in bed, shaking fiercely. He grabbed his most prized possession, his fiddle, and hugged it to him, hiding himself under his blankets until only his eyes showed. He stared in terror at the bolted door as the footsteps came down the hall.

The bolted door burst open with a loud bang, and a dark figure stepped through, bringing silence with him. The sound of the wind and the rain was blotted out in an instant, and in the eerie stillness, Matthews made out a tall man in a steeple-crowned hat, corselet, jackboots, and a flowing cloak. A sword hung at his side.

Matthews opened and closed his mouth in terror, but no sound came forth. The dark figure towered above the bed, glowing slightly in the blackness of the room, and stared down into the shaking fiddler's eyes.

"I am Peter Printz, the governor-general of this land," the apparition announced in a voice that sent shivers racing through Matthews' body. "Tonight is the autumnal equinox, and my friends have come from far and wide for a dance. You will play your fiddle for us."

Again, Matthews opened his mouth to speak, but the ghost cut him off with a sharp gesture of warning: "You are not to speak a word, fiddler. Say nothing at all this night, or it will go hard with you. Just bring thy fiddle and come to the dance."

Matthews' body rose from the mattress without his conscious volition. He followed the phosphorous figure through the door, down the stairs, and along the hallway, his fiddle clutched to his chest. The only sound was the thud of the phantom's boot heels. Doors flew open as the governor-general approached, and the

THE LAST DANCE

glowing figure walked arrogantly through each one until he came to the reception room, where all the dances were once held.

The reception room was aglow with light and laughter. Candles stood on every surface and gleamed in a huge chandelier in the ceiling, their flames shining brilliantly from many mirrors and from the smooth, waxed floor. A great fire burned and snapped in the hearth, and portraits and tapestries shone brightly, as if newly created. A hundred glowing men and women arrayed in the elegant attire of days of yore mingled and laughed, drank and spoke together, flirted, bowed, curtseyed, and accepted drinks from liveried servants. Matthews was stunned and paused uncertainly in the doorway.

At the appearance of the governor-general, the room became silent, and the phosphorous forms of the men and women bowed and curtseyed in respect. Then their semitransparent eyes slid past Printz and focused on the solid, unimaginative form of the fiddler standing with his instrument clutched to his heart. Matthews fumbled for the flask of whiskey he kept attached to his belt, and he took a fortifying pull. The reflexive gesture brought a hollow laugh from a hundred ghostly throats. Matthews flushed painfully and put the flask away.

"Play," Governor-General Printz commanded, pointing a glowing finger toward a chair in the corner.

Matthews scurried to the chair, tuned the strings, and put his fiddle beneath his chin with shaking fingers. He struck the first notes of a jig, and immediately, the ghostly guests joined hands and began to dance. Their dance was merry and informal, almost flirtatious. The women circled the men, and their partners leaped high, clicking their heels and performing magnificent feats.

Matthews played faster and still faster as the whiskey worked its way into his blood.

Through the uncanny silence that lay over the whole house, Matthews could faintly make out the wild sounds of the storm raging outside. The dancing couples in front of him whipped about and whirled as wildly as the wind that buffeted the house. Matthews had never played the fiddle so well in his life, though he did not recognize any of the tunes that his fingers plucked from the strings.

Matthews never knew how long he played for the phantoms of Printz Hall. As suddenly as it started, it was over. Governor-General Printz loomed at the center of the glittering room and held up his hands for silence. "You have played well, fiddler, and so shalt thou be paid."

The ghost gestured to his servants, and they brought forth a large strongbox that was filled to the brim with gold pieces.

"Hold out thy fiddle bag," Printz commanded. Dazed by the sight of so much gold, Matthews did as he was told. The governor-general began heaping handfuls of treasure into the bag, while Matthews watched with open-mouthed astonishment. At the fourth handful, the fiddler, forgetting his injunction to remain silent, shouted: "Lord Almighty! Here's luck!"

Instantly, the room was filled with a terrible shriek that started low and rose so high that it buzzed through the skull and caused intense pain. Through the horrible scream, Matthews saw all the candles flare up. Demonic laughter sounded from a hundred throats. The fiddle in his hands shattered, and the lights snuffed out in a brilliant flash, leaving the room in darkness. Matthews fell to the floor and blacked out.

He awoke to see brilliant light streaming in through a broken window pane and the anxious face of his best friend Joseph bent over him. Matthews sat up abruptly and reached for his fiddle. To his dismay, he saw that it lay in a thousand tiny pieces upon the floor. "Where's my money?" he gasped to his friend, reaching for the green fiddle bag at his side. It was empty.

"What happened?" asked Joseph anxiously. Matthews shook his head, wordless. He stared blankly around the dusk-covered reception room with its broken windows, tattered tapestries, and ripped portraits. The hearth seemed to mock him with its emptiness, and in his mind, he heard the terrible screaming sound and saw the flashing of the candles.

"Lord Almighty!" he shouted in sudden fear. He leaped to his feet and ran out of the reception room, out of the mansion, and all the way home. Joseph paused only long enough to collect his friend's belongings and then followed the fiddler to his house, where he demanded, and was given, the whole story. Joseph averred that it was probably a good thing that his friend did not accept the demon money, and Matthews, with a sad look at the remains of his shattered fiddle, reluctantly agreed.

The old Printz mansion burned to the ground the very next night. Matthews believed to his dying day that it was the ghosts who set it on fire, using the coals from the hearth of the reception room. Two days later, a beautiful new fiddle appeared on Matthews' doorstep, with no card or letter attached to it. But the fiddler knew it came from Quidd, and Matthews ever after played all the Quaker's favorite songs whenever the man came into the tavern to drink with his friends.

6

Ghost in the Steel Mill

PITTSBURGH

His lame leg prevented him from serving in the army when World War II broke out in Europe. That didn't stop him from trying to help out in any way he could. For decades, his family had worked a farm just outside Pittsburgh. One day shortly after the United States joined the war, the farmer packed a satchel full of clothes and went to town to find a job in Jones and Laughlin Steel Corporation's Number 2 Shop at the Southside steel mill complex. Pittsburgh had become the Arsenal of Democracy for World War II, producing steel not just for America, but also for its allies, and he wanted to be a part of the effort.

The farmer found it difficult to adjust to his new life. The pollution was terrible. Thick black smoke choked the skies, forcing people to drive their cars with headlights on at noon in order to see where they were going. Chemicals from the factories spewed into the river, where it mixed with untreated human waste. There were dead fish everywhere, and the farmer was appalled when he discovered that the river water was being pumped back into the city untreated as drinking water for homes and businesses.

Worst to his mind was the large number of people crammed into his community. The farmer was almost never alone: Mothers, fathers, children, single workers, old folks, and the young were everywhere he turned. They got on his nerves after the open spaces and sparse neighborhood in the farmlands of his home. He hated living in ill-housed, overworked, disorganized, and generally squalid Pittsburgh. Folks called it "Hell with the Lid Off," and he heartily agreed with their sentiments. Still, he was doing his bit for the country, and that helped soothe his pride, which was regularly hurt by the limitations of his lame leg.

The farmer was put to work in the melt shop and soon learned to be very careful around the furnace and the ladles full of molten steel. The other workers often spoke about Joe Macarac, the ultimate steel hero of folklore whose exploits were akin to those of Paul Bunyan. According to the workers, Macarac not only drank hot steel for soup, he could also scoop it up in his bare hands and form it into horseshoes and cannonballs. Macarac once caught a falling ladle full of molten steel with his bare hands, easing it safely to the ground and saving the lives of his crew. This piece of folklore comforted the men, the farmer knew, since every worker feared what would happen if the chains holding the ladles full of molten steel ever broke while they passed overhead. Burning to death in molten steel might be a quick demise, but it would be agonizing.

This was the reason that the tale of the ghost in the steel mill, while complete fiction in the farmer's opinion, was still heart-wrenching and horrible. Apparently, a man named Jim Grabowski tripped over a rigger hose back in 1922 and fell into a ladle of hot steel. His body was immediately liquefied; there was nothing

GHOST IN THE STEEL MILL

left for his family to bury save for a small nugget of steel that was skimmed from the tainted ladle before its contents were dumped into a vacant lot. From that day onward, the workers said that Jim's ghost clanked its way around 2 Shop at night, searching for his dead body. Some men claimed to have heard the ghost screaming in agony as he relived his final moments. The screams were shortly followed by the maniacal laughter of the ghost, whose mind had gone mad with the pain of his death.

The farmer was not afraid of the ghost. He thought the story was as much a tall tale as the exploits of Joe Macarac. When other men shied away from night work in the melt shop, he volunteered to take their shifts. He liked the extra money this earned him, and soon his reputation for fearlessness and his scorn for the ghost of Jim Grabowski were the talk of the mill.

There came an evening when the farmer found himself alone on the furnace floor. It was the slow time between shifts, and by rights he should already be on his way home. However, he had stayed behind for a moment to complete a small task, and he hummed contentedly to himself as he bent over his work. He gradually became aware of a muffled sound coming from somewhere to his left. He ignored it, since the mechanized processes all around him often made strange sounds.

The sound grew louder, and the farmer finally looked up from his labors to see a glowing white mist gathering in the air a few yards away from where he stood. The mist emitted a faint rapping noise, which slowly clarified into the steady thud of approaching footsteps.

The farmer gasped, goose bumps forming on his arms in spite of the heat from the furnace. He watched with unblinking eyes as the mist solidified into the glowing figure of a workman making his rounds. Suddenly, the man tripped and fell downward in slow motion toward a shimmering ladle full of steaming molten steel. The phantom workman's body plunged into the hot liquid, and he tried in vain to grab the sides of the ladle and pull himself out, unwilling to believe that he was doomed. Then, his body liquefying and his face hideously twisted with pain, the ghostly workman screamed desperately for someone to save him as he sank downward into the red-hot ladle. With a final, hair-raising shriek, the apparition disappeared.

The farmer's own scream of sheer terror was so loud that it cut through the voice of the phantom, echoing and reechoing through the furnace room. Dropping his tools as if he himself were burning up, the farmer raced for the exit as fast as his lame leg would take him, the gut-wrenching sound of maniacal laughter behind him.

He ran all the way home, packed his satchel, and set out at once for his home. The farmer stopped just long enough to inform his boss that he was quitting, then limped down the smoke-filled roads toward the outskirts of town, thumbing for a lift whenever he saw a pair of headlights pierce the smoggy dawn. He never looked back.

The farmer spent the rest of the war growing crops and providing food for those who labored in the steel mills. He always sent a representative into Pittsburgh with his produce rather than venture into that terrible, phantom-filled city again. Once was enough.

7

Death on the Spur

OLD LOGGER'S PATH
TIADAGHTON STATE FOREST,
LYCOMING COUNTY

"Aaaaaaaaaaaaaaaah!"

The scream cut through the early evening activities of the lumber camp, immediately halting all activity. The smell of newly cut timber laced with the scent of gently bubbling stew had drawn most of the men toward the main encampment in search of their supper. All heads in the mess line turned toward the sound, and the experienced lumberjacks all grinned, exchanging nudges and smiles.

"Looks like someone just met our ghosts," Red MacPherson said to his friend Jack.

"Yep. Young Harley," Jack said, pointing toward a sandy-haired, slender lad who was running down the path that led to the railroad spur used for hauling away lumber.

Harley skidded to a halt in front of the two men. He was pale and shaking with fright.

"I just saw. . . I just saw. . . " he gasped. "You won't believe what I just saw!"

"A ghost?" Red asked casually.

"Two ghosts, I think," said Jack, accepting a bowl of stew from the cook and stepping out of the line.

Harley gaped at him. "Yes! Yes! Two ghosts. How did you know?"

"Why do you think the lumber camp and the railroad have such difficulty keeping employees?" asked Red, expertly snagging two pieces of bread to dip in his stew. He commandeered a second bowl for poor, pale Harley and guided him over to a seat. "Most men abandon the place as soon as they set eyes upon the ghosts," Red continued, shaking his head sadly. "Young folks these days just don't have any backbone."

"Tell us what you saw, lad," Jack said as he slurped contentedly at his stew.

Harley twitched a bit, and his left hand, which held his stew bowl, began to shake. Red patted the young man on the shoulder and urged him to take a deep breath. After inhaling a few times, Harley's hand steadied, and he began his tale.

It was dusk, and Harley had been out marking a stand of trees that were due for cutting in the next week. The stand was near the railroad spur, and Harley had sprinted up to the railroad tracks to make the long walk back to the camp, preferring the smooth tracks of the railroad to the rough ground of the forest.

While he strolled along, Harley felt a prickling sensation on the back of his neck, as if someone of ill intent were staring at him. He shivered, glancing around, but did not see anyone else on the tracks. There were plenty of shadows in the dark woods to either side, though, and someone might easily be hiding just a few feet from where he walked. Harley picked up his pace. He didn't think he had any enemies in the lumber camp, but it might be a wanderer or a thief.

Suddenly, a flash of light as bright as the sun exploded into being directly in front of him. Harley staggered backward, covering his eyes for a moment against the blinding glare. The air around him turned cold, as if the light were made of ice, and he fell to his knees in fear. For a moment, a thousand little sparkles like too-bright fireflies danced around and around the railroad tracks. Then they faded a bit, consolidating into one large mass.

Slowly, Harley dropped his arm and gazed in fear and amazement upon the glowing figure of a massive man dressed in the rough working clothes he associated with gandy dancers, those railroad employees who replaced rotten cross ties and were responsible for keeping the rails aligned. There was a look of swaggering, vicious triumph on the face of the phantom man, who was gazing down upon a glowing heap at his feet. The massive ghost slowly set down his pick and kicked at the heap. Harley realized with horror that it was the corpse of another gandy dancer. The corpse had a bloody hole in the side of his head. A glance at the dripping end of the tall man's pick told Harley the grisly truth: The corpse had been murdered by his fellow employee.

The massive gandy dancer moved a few steps away, searching for something. Harley kept a wary eye on the phantom as he moved. When the ghost returned, he was pushing a glowing wheelbarrow before him. The gandy dancer lifted the corpse easily, tossing it into the wheelbarrow so that the dead man's bloody head lolled over one side and his feet dangled over the other. Then the ghostly railroad worker pushed the wheelbarrow along

DEATH ON THE SPUR

the track, singing one of the gandy dancer's call-and-response work songs that were used to ease the pain of hard labor and keep all the laborers in rhythm as they levered the heavy track.

> *"Pick an' shovel . . . huh,*
> *am so heavy . . . huh,*
> *Heavy as lead . . . huh,*
> *heavy as lead . . . huh*
> *Pickin', shov'lin' . . . huh*
> *pickin', shov'lin' . . . huh*
> *Till I'm dead . . . huh*
> *till I'm dead . . . "*

The murderer sang the words cheerfully as he pushed the phantom wheelbarrow off the track and down toward the woods to dump his victim. At the edge of the trees, the ghosts disappeared.

It was only then that Harley, released from his frozen terror, let out a terrible scream and went running down the tracks to the lumber camp.

Harley was sweating with fear by the time he finished his story. Red handed him a tankard of ale, and he downed it all in one go.

"Well done, lad," Jack said, patting his arm. "You are one of the few who stayed long enough to see the phantoms. Most fellows bolt when they see the flash of light."

"Who are they?" asked Harley with a tremble in his voice.

"Railroad workers who argued while building the railroad spur," Red said. "That's what I heard."

"Gandy dancers arguing over a girl, is the story I was told," Jack countered. "One murdered the other while they were out alone fixing a few broken ties on the spur."

"Whichever version you believe, the ghosts have been seen many times at dusk, reenacting the events following the murder," said Red.

"Was the dead man ever found? Was the murderer ever punished?" asked Harley.

"Yes to both," said Jack promptly. "Some of the old timers still remember the day the body was discovered and the arrest and trial that followed. There was never much doubt about who did it, and none at all after the murderer was hanged and his ghost started appearing on the tracks."

Harley gave a final shudder, then rose with his empty bowl. "Well, I don't aim to give up a good job on account of a few ghosts," he said. He pulled a rag out of his pocket and wiped his sweaty forehead. "On the other hand, I don't aim to be walking the railroad spur at night after this! The woods are good enough for me."

The two older men chuckled as he walked away.

"A fine, brave lad," Jack said, and Red agreed.

8

Ben and Me

PHILADELPHIA

I've raised a passel of children in my time, and there's not a bad one in the lot, if I do say so myself. Full of high spirits they were, too, always running and shouting and playing. But I never took any cheek from my young ones, no sir! As soon as any of them started mouthing off, I gave them what's what, and they never tried it again. So it stands to reason that I wasn't going to take any cheek from a ghost either, not even a famous one like the ghost of Ben Franklin.

I was working for the library in those days, doing the early morning cleaning before the library opened. This worked out well for us; my man watched the young ones while I was out, and I took over for him a few minutes before his day job started. This allowed us the evenings free to spend with our children.

My eldest girl came to the library with me sometimes to help tidy up the place. It was the first subscription library in America, started by no less a person than Ben Franklin himself (though that was before my time), and I was right proud to be a part of such a fine institution. We took great care cleaning and polishing and dusting so that the place sparkled each morning when the doors opened for subscribers.

It was a week after I took the job that I first bumped into the ghost. I was polishing the woodwork on one of the bookcases when I felt a cool breeze on the back of my neck. Wondering if one of the windows had been left open by mistake, I turned and saw the glowing form of a cheerful, balding man wearing a simple jacket, waistcoat, and breeches that were worn by working class men in the early 1800s. He was walking toward me, carrying a pile of books in his arms, and I gasped aloud, recognizing his face from statues I had seen all over the city. It was Ben Franklin.

I was frozen in amazement but felt no fear of this happy apparition. He passed me, and his phantom body was so close I could have reached out and touched him, had I wished. I most emphatically did not so wish, but I did watch until he disappeared through a doorway.

Slowly, I turned back to my work, but I couldn't concentrate. Leaving my dust rags by the bookcase, I went to the door and looked into the room where the ghost had disappeared. He wasn't there. Disappointed, I returned to my dusting.

After that first early morning, I began to see the ghost of Benjamin Franklin regularly as I went about my cleaning. He would carry books from room to room, climb ladders to reach high shelves, talk silently but animatedly to himself as he paced back and forth across the floor, and bend over a table full of papers, deep in thought. He never took any notice of me, and I left him strictly alone.

My eldest daughter was intrigued by the phantom. Whenever she accompanied me to work, she would eagerly await the arrival of the ghost and would break off what she was doing to follow him around the library. Then she would hurry back to me and give me a detailed report on his activities as I dusted and scrubbed and polished. After a few days of this, I curtailed her phantom following in favor of real-life dusting, and things went back to normal.

Although I never admitted it to my daughter, I too was intrigued by the specter of Benjamin Franklin that haunted the library. I knew he had been one of the most prominent of our founding fathers, but I knew very little more. I was a firm believer in self-education, often staying up late to read books I had borrowed from this very library, so I took out a book about him.

I learned from his autobiography that Benjamin Franklin was born in Boston, Massachusetts, where he was apprenticed to his brother, who was a printer. Unhappy at home, Ben ran away from his apprenticeship and moved to Philadelphia, where he eventually became a newspaper editor, printer, and merchant. Ben Franklin was the publisher of the famous *Poor Richard's Almanac* and the *Pennsylvania Gazette*. Not only had he founded the first public lending library in America, but he also started the first fire department and a political discussion club.

Franklin was noted for his curiosity, ingenuity, and diversity of interests. His wit and wisdom were proverbial. He was a leader of the Enlightenment and had the attention of scientists and intellectuals all across Europe. His experiments with electricity were legendary. He invented the lightning rod, Franklin stove, medical catheter, swim fins, glass harmonica, and bifocals. He was a noted linguist, who was fluent in five languages, and he even took an interest in astrology.

BEN AND ME

More than anyone, Ben Franklin shaped the American Revolution, though I was surprised to learn that he never held a national elective office. As an agent in London before the revolution, and later as a minister to France during the conflict, Franklin helped define the new nation in the minds of Europeans, inventing the notion of colonial unity and the idea of America. His success in securing French military and financial aid was decisive for American victory over Britain.

I was impressed by the life of old Ben Franklin and treated his ghost with respect tinged with awe. I had no idea why he had chosen to return to the library he started, but he was company of a sort, and so we passed many a morning together, happily ignoring each other as we went about our various tasks.

One day, I was down on my knees scrubbing industriously away at the floor in front of a bookcase long favored by Ben Franklin when the phantom himself came around the corner with a load of books in his arms. Hastily, I sprang to my feet and started gathering my pails and brushes, not wanting to interfere with the ghost's self-appointed task.

As I gathered up my gear, the phantom started tapping his toe impatiently and shifting his books from one arm to the other. "Just one moment," I told him as I searched for a recalcitrant brush that had slipped under the bookcase. At that moment, the ghost bumped into me, thrusting me out of his way. It was quite a solid thump. It nearly knocked me over, and the chill I got from the touch of his spectral form nearly froze me to death. Once I was out of his way, the ghost stepped up to the bookcase and deposited his armload of tomes on the top shelf.

Well, that did it. I don't take any cheek from my children,

and I certainly wasn't going to take it from a ghost, especially not from the respectable specter of a founding father. I straightened to my full five foot six inches and glared at the ghost.

"Just who do you think you are?" I demanded, thrusting a finger under his nose. The phantom was clearly taken aback.

"I'm ashamed of you!" I continued. "An intelligent, well-read gentleman such as yourself should have better manners than that! Bumping into a lady! Well, really! Were you raised in a barn?"

The ghost of Ben Franklin looked abashed and backed away, shoulders slumping and head down. I followed him down the hall, lecturing him all the while on politeness to a lady, patience as a cardinal virtue, the proper behavior of a phantom founding father, ghostly etiquette in general terms, and my true opinion of the lightning rod.

My eldest daughter came running to see what had set me off and stared in amazement at the sight of the ghost scurrying down the hall in an attempt to shake me off. But I backed him into a corner and continued my lecture until I had completely voiced my ire. Finally, the ghost of Ben Franklin held his hands palms up in his most placating manner, then placed them together in a prayerful attitude and bowed low to me in apology.

"Well, all right then," I said grudgingly. "Just don't do it again."

Ben Franklin's ghost nodded fervently and then vanished through the wall.

After that, the ghost never gave me any trouble. In fact, he started avoiding any room in which I was working. I often saw him peeking around corners to see if I was anywhere close by before entering a room, and he scuttled in the opposite direction if he saw me coming down the hallway. As I said before, I don't take cheek from anybody, not even a ghost. Ben Franklin learned that the hard way.

9

The Toy Room

ALLENTOWN

A retired couple had always wanted to live in a Victorian-style home and were thrilled when a beautiful old house went on the market in their hometown. It had been built in the mid-1800s and had remained in the family of the builder for several generations, but now the owners were forced to sell. The house was right in the couple's price range, too, and as the wife said, they might never get another chance like this. So they put in a bid on the house and were thrilled when it was quickly accepted.

When they were closing on the house, the wife jokingly asked if the house had a ghost. The owner, an elderly woman, smiled and said that a ghost had never bothered her, but that there was a sad death associated with the house.

One summer day, the woman told them, around a hundred years ago, the family dog had leaped off the porch and into the yard in pursuit of the neighbor's cat. The little girl of the house had pursued immediately, intent on saving the poor bedeviled cat, and had tripped over the small, ornamental wire fence that surrounded her mother's peony plant in the front yard. The rusty wire had punctured her bare right foot, causing a small wound. Thinking nothing of it, the little girl had captured the dog and gone back to her play. But she soon developed tetanus, which turned to lockjaw, and the poor girl had died in the upstairs room that was now used as a bathroom.

After they closed on the house, the husband moved in immediately, while his wife stayed on in their old house until it sold six weeks later. The couple was pleased with their new home. It had a large attic and a wonderfully crooked staircase. The front stairs led to a wide-open area from which one could access the three bedrooms and the bath. The downstairs had a huge kitchen, a beautiful dining room, and two spacious parlors.

As was always the case in an old house, there were many things that needed to be updated or replaced. The roof needed repairs, the plumbing was out-of-date, and the radiators did not always function correctly. Fortunately, it was summertime when they closed on the house, and they decided not to worry about the radiators until the fall, when the heat would be turned on for the first time. Instead, the husband concentrated on the plumbing and on fixing up a few other things that needed more immediate attention, while the wife set about furnishing the spacious rooms. She scoured the local flea markets for antiques and other items with which to fill every nook and cranny, in the traditional Victorian style.

Over the summer, as the wife transformed the old house into a home, odd things began to occur. Items were moved or knocked over when nobody was home. The radiators in the upstairs bathroom and in the spacious upstairs hallway began to make loud thumping sounds in the middle of the night, even though the furnace remained off. It sounded as if someone were rapping a fist against the metal in anger. Then the unwound, ornamental clocks in the upstairs bedrooms began to toll in the middle of the night. Bong, bong, bong; the clocks would strike seven times in a row and then cease as abruptly as they started.

The husband slept peacefully through the nightly racket, but the wife started awake each time the radiator thumped or the unwound clocks rang. The activity seemed to center around the bathroom and the hallway. Sometimes the wife would come out of their bedroom and turn on the lights to see if she could find a cause for the noise, but no one was there.

Then a cold spot developed in the bathroom, causing the wife to shiver each time she entered. Suddenly she remembered the story of the little girl who lived and died in that very room. Was it the child who had come back to haunt her old home? Was she unhappy because strangers had moved in?

In the fall the wife began to transform the spacious upper hallway into a toy room for her grandchildren. She lined the walls with cases and filled them with dolls and books and soft toys. She put a rocking horse in a corner and set up a small tea table and chairs in the center of the hall. A trunk full of play clothes went next to the tea table, and across from it was a cushioned rocking chair that was suitable for any adult who might want to watch over the children as they played. Beside the window stood a magnificent, three-story dollhouse that was papered and carpeted and filled with everything a little girl's heart could desire.

The night after the dollhouse was placed in the toy room, the wife awakened to the sound of small doors opening and shutting in the dollhouse. The rocking horse creaked, and then she heard

THE TOY ROOM

the sound of happy humming. Slipping out of bed, she crept to the door and looked out into the toy room. Moonlight was streaming through the window, and in its glow she saw a doll floating sideways a few feet above the floor, as if it were being carried underneath someone's arm. The doll was carefully set in one of the small chairs at the tea table, and another doll soon joined it. A large teddy bear occupied the third chair, and a moment later, teacups were carefully placed in front of each guest. The fourth chair was pulled out, and then a teacup was lifted to an invisible mouth. The wife could hear polite but indistinct chatter coming from the transparent hostess of the tea party. When the meal was over, the dolls were carefully returned to their places by the humming hostess. With a last affectionate pat on the rocking horse's head, the room became empty, save for the watching wife.

After that night, the angry thumping ceased, there were no more unexplained messes, and anything that disappeared was easily attributed to her husband's refusal to wear his glasses except when he was reading. The wife got a picture of the little girl from the previous owner of the house, put it in a frame, and placed it in the toy room. Though she never saw the ghost at play again, occasionally one of the unwound clocks would strike seven times in a row, and once in a while, when no one else was around, the wife could hear a happy humming sound coming from the toy room.

10

Old Coaly

I had no idea, when I first moved into Watts Hall, that my new dorm was haunted. I mean, almost every state university has stories about ghosts in the dormitories, so I wasn't surprised to hear about a phantom on campus. However, usually the stories involve some poor soul who committed suicide or a founder of the college who returned to his old stomping grounds for auld lang syne. I didn't expect to find the phantom of a pack mule kicking around the premises, which was why I was astonished one day when I wandered into the basement, heading for the study lounge, and found the hall occupied by a very large mule.

"What are you doing here?" I asked the creature. Obviously, someone was playing some sort of prank and had stashed the mule down here for safekeeping. The mule lowered its oversized ears and blinked placidly at me. I put my books down on a desk and wandered over to rub the mule on the head. It liked the attention and leaned its head against me so hard that it almost knocked me over. Then it vanished. I let out a shout of sheer astonishment, which brought a fellow student running into the hall.

"There. . . there. . . there. . . " I stuttered. I tried again. "Mule. . . mule. . . mule. . . "

I swallowed and tried one last time: "It just vanished!" I cried, waving my arms in the air for emphasis.

At once, the student's face lit up with understanding, and he laughed. "Oh, that's just the ghost of Old Coaly," he said.

"Old Coaly?" I asked, still shaking with the shock of the mule's disappearance.

According to my informant, Old Coaly helped to build the original five-story Old Main building. He and his owner's son, Andy Lytle, were recruited on a day-hire status after moving to Pennsylvania from Kentucky in 1857. They were among the 200 workers who helped to construct the original Old Main, located about the same place Old Main stands today. The mule's job was to haul limestone to the construction site from a quarry located near what is now the intersection of College Avenue and Pugh Street.

After construction was completed in 1863, the university purchased Old Coaly for $190 (at the time a very high price indeed) and offered him a home on Old Main lawn, which was then a farm. Old Coaly spent his next thirty years helping the farmers and assisting with construction projects on campus. The students were very fond of the mule. Sometimes, as a prank, they would take Old Coaly up to the top of Old Main's bell tower and leave him up there for a few hours. It made them laugh to hear his bray ringing out over the campus from the rooftop.

In fact, my informant continued, the students loved the mule so much that he was deemed Penn State's first unofficial mascot. When Old Coaly died of natural causes on January 1, 1893, the students decided to preserve his skeleton and display it in Old Main. After a fire in the early 1900s, Old Coaly's remains were temporarily stored in the basement of Watts Hall, before his skeleton was put on display in the 1960s at the Agricultural Building. Old Coaly was finally moved to the HUB-Robeson Center as part of Penn State's sesquicentennial celebration.

Ever since Old Coaly's remains came to Watts Hall, students had heard strange braying noises coming from the storage room where the bones were kept. I was not the first to see Old Coaly standing in the hallway, the student concluded, nodding his head decisively for emphasis. He seemed to think it was quite an honor for me to have seen the Watts Hall ghost and wanted to drag me around campus so I could tell the story to all his friends. I declined with the excuse that I needed to get ready for a date and hurried back to my room, my head aswirl with all the information I had just learned.

Why, I wondered, had the ghost appeared to me? Was it because I came from a long line of farmers? Or did it have something to do with the second sight that had been handed down to me from my Scottish forebears? My hand still felt oily from the rough hair of the mule, and Old Coaly's pungent smell was still in my nostrils. He had felt so real. . . .

Apparently, I became a favorite of Old Coaly. Whenever I entered the basement of Watts Hall, the storage closet would echo with his excited brays. If I remained downstairs for any length of time, he would appear in the hallway and try to squeeze himself through the door of the study lounge. I was the only one

OLD COALY

who could actually see the ghost, and I didn't say anything about my ability after that first day, since I didn't want people to think I was crazy.

Although I grumbled to myself about the ghostly mule, I always kept a few carrots in my pocket, and I would give them to Old Coaly whenever I saw him in the hallway. We would stand together for a few moments while I scratched his ears and he crunched contentedly, but he would always disappear if he heard another student approaching. His affectionate displays were just for me.

Toward the end of the semester, as finals loomed closer, I spent less and less time in the basement with Old Coaly. The phantom mule did not like that. He took to braying long and loudly whenever he knew I was in the building. His noisy complaints were so frequent that even those who were not attuned to the occult began to hear him.

The evening before my last final was particularly difficult. I am not normally a light sleeper, but for some reason I tossed and turned in my bed long past 2:00 A.M. Usually, I could ignore Old Coaly's braying, knowing that after an hour or so he would settle down and amble away to munch in whatever green pastures were available to phantom mules. But that night, Old Coaly's braying combined with the howl of a huge thunderstorm to keep me awake.

The situation was getting dire. I had a 9:00 final, and if I didn't get some rest, I was going to sleep right through my exam. Finally, I jumped out of bed and stormed down to the basement. Old Coaly heard me coming and stuck his head right through the center of the storage room door to greet me, giving him the appearance of a stuffed and mounted moose head.

"If I fail that exam tomorrow, you are going to be one sorry mule!" I told him, waving my finger sternly under his nose. Old Coaly whickered unrepentantly and trotted right through the solid mass of the door and into the hall. He began nuzzling me, looking for carrots, but I hadn't brought any. I scratched his ears for a moment, finding it hard to remain angry with such an affectionate beast. Then I slapped his side and ordered him back into the storage closet. What could you do?

I was going home for the winter break right after my exam the next day, but I stopped down to see Old Coaly one last time. I told him I was moving into an off-campus apartment next semester, but that I would drop in now and then to see him. I am not sure if he understood me, but he seemed content enough to crunch his carrot and then amble back through the storage room door.

As I left the dorm, I heard a happy bray coming from the basement. Perhaps, I mused as I unlocked my car and got into the driver's seat, Old Coaly would find another student to give him carrots next semester. If he didn't, I might end up with the ghost of a mule haunting my second-floor apartment!

The Flood

JOHNSTOWN

For many generations, all of the women in my family have been psychic. My grandmother dreamed dreams that came true. My sister's premonitions were always accurate, and my mother was a true clairvoyant, who never took money for her readings and only gave them to friends and family. Even my brother was spot-on accurate with his predictions concerning who would win the local football games and other sporting events.

I, on the other hand, turned out to be as psychic as your average oyster—which is not psychic at all. This was a source of great astonishment to my family. To compensate, I became an over-achiever who made wonderful grades, was the homecoming queen three years straight, and went on to achieve a modicum of greatness in my chosen field of work. Still, while very proud of my academic and social achievements, my family always treated me as if I were missing a limb. I found this very irritating, but what could I do? I couldn't change who I was! I lay the blame on my father, whose family had absolutely no psi abilities what-soever. My father and I would hang out together during family parties, two of a kind, while the rest of the family discussed their latest premonitions, readings, and other psychic topics of that ilk.

My father was a history buff who loved to visit historic sites. One day, when my family planned a prolonged get-together to discuss some serious readings my mother had done for a cousin, my father and I decided to take a jaunt together over to Johnstown, which was about an hour away from the old homestead, to check out the history museum and read up on the terrible flood that had devastated the town in 1889.

It was a lovely day, and we enjoyed the beautiful drive. Johnstown, I knew from my reading, had been built into a river valley on the Appalachian Plateau. The Little Conemaugh and Stony Creek Rivers ran along the peripheral edge of the town and merged to form the Conemaugh River at the western end. At least once a year, one or both of the rivers overflowed due to heavy rain or snow melt, and the town's residents would scurry to protect what they could of their homes and their belongings.

As we drove into town, I was struck by a sudden chill and groped in the backseat for my sweater. Though the summer day was hot and sunny, I couldn't stop shivering. Just at the edge of my hearing was a soft murmur like that of sad voices almost out of reach. I clutched the folds of the sweater around me and laughingly told my father that a goose had walked over my grave. He chuckled and said, "Now, don't you go psychic on me, Patty. Three psychics in our family are enough."

"Four, if you count Grandma," I replied with a grin.

Our first stop was the Johnstown Flood Museum, which was located in a building that Andrew Carnegie had built for the town after the original library was destroyed in the flood. There we learned all about that horrible day—May 31, 1889—when, high in the mountains above Johnstown, the South Fork Dam collapsed suddenly after a phenomenal storm roared for eleven hours over the area, dumping a massive amount of rain on the beleaguered land below. Officials had feared the old dam holding back the 2-mile-long Lake Conemaugh would fail and had worked to avoid this by adding height to the dam, digging a second spillway to relieve pressure, and releasing the heavy screens placed on the overflows to keep the stocked fish from escaping into the streams below.

The official's fears were justified when, just after 3:00 P.M., the dam gave way, releasing 20 million tons of water into the valley. The deluge rushed down the narrow gorge of the Conemaugh River, which was already swollen by the heavy rains. Within the hour, a body of water, which engineers at the time estimated moved into the valley with the force of Niagara Falls, rolled into Johnstown with 14 miles of accumulated debris, including houses, barns, animals, and people, dead and alive. Few residents saw the approaching wave, but everyone heard the thunderous rumble of the flood as it swept into the city, picking up people, houses, animals, and other detritus and taking it all for a wild ride through the town and down to the Pennsylvania Railroad Company's Stone Bridge.

At the Old Stone Bridge, the flood waters, clogged with houses, animals, bodies, and trees, formed a huge whirlpool. Debris was piled 40 feet high and spread over thirty acres, and it quickly caught fire. Some people were swept past the bridge and shot down the Conemaugh River to die or be rescued at other communities downstream. More than two thousand people died

THE FLOOD

that day in the catastrophic flood, including ninety-nine entire families and 396 children. Bodies of flood victims were found as far away as Cincinnati, Ohio.

I was stunned at the photos on display at the museum and by the documentary about the flood. Four square miles of downtown Johnstown was completely obliterated. Sixteen hundred homes were destroyed, and $17 million in property damage was done, amazing figures for the time period. Flood lines were found as high as 89 feet above river level, and the great wave itself measured 35 to 40 feet high and hit Johnstown at 40 miles per hour. The force of the flood swept several locomotives weighing 170,000 pounds as far as 4,800 feet.

What moved me most was the representation of an "Oklahoma" house, which was one of the first types of temporary houses erected to shelter the people left homeless by the flood. How wrenching it must have been to have lost one's home with all its memories and mementos and suddenly find oneself living in a 10-by-20-foot shelter. And these were the lucky people whose lives were spared.

The dead had been lined up in morgues throughout the city and in many other communities farther down the river, waiting for survivors to come and identify them. The living set up tents, often near the places their former homes had been located, and began the difficult task of cleaning up and starting over.

Clara Barton and the Red Cross arrived from Washington, D.C.; she helped to build hotels for people to live in and set up warehouses in which to store the clothing, food, medicines, bandages, and lumber sent from all over the country once word of the flood hit the newspapers. The Cambria Iron Company began anew on June 6, and by July 1 many Johnstown stores reopened for business on Main Street.

Tearing ourselves reluctantly from the exhibits, my father and I exited the museum to take a walking tour through the town. As soon as my feet hit the pavement, my shivers returned. I put my sweater back on but did not say anything to my father about the sad, murmuring voices I heard, though they were louder now.

When we paused at the First Methodist Episcopal Church, which not only had survived the flood, but had also sheltered several buildings behind it, I heard a roaring sound as loud as the thunder of a mighty cataract. Out of the corner of my eye, I caught sight of a rolling hill of detritus about 40 feet high and a half-mile wide rushing toward me. I gave a startled shriek of terror as it slammed into the church beside me, the churning, swirling water tearing around and through the building. I whirled to get a closer look at the flooded church, but there was nothing there.

My father stopped in mid-sentence and stared at me. "What's wrong? Were you stung by a bee?" he asked.

I shook my head, too shocked to say anything. I tried to grin. "Nothing's wrong," I finally managed. "I just remember that I forgot to mail a bill that was due yesterday."

After peering at me sharply for a moment or two, my father resumed his lecture about the church.

When we reached Alma Hall, where 264 people took shelter during the flood, I thought I heard the sound of a woman sobbing and exclamations of terror from several male voices. I kept looking behind me, thinking it must be a group of tourists who were taking the walking tour, but no one was there. My father gave me a strange look but said nothing about my fidgeting.

It was when we reached the Presbyterian church that I knew something strange was happening to me. I could smell the pungent stink of death, decay, and rot from halfway down the street. My father didn't have to tell me that the place had been used as a morgue. As soon as I entered the building, I could see the scene as clearly as if I had been there.

The first floor of the church had been completely washed out, and the water had also submerged and badly damaged the second floor. Pews, floors, and walls were still damp and dripping, while the carpets were buried an inch deep in stinking mud. Undertakers and their assistants were slipping and sliding as they walked through the chancel, which was full of coffins, strips of muslin, and the other accoutrements of the undertaking profession.

Through the stench of the mud and mildew, I saw a dozen pine boxes lying across the top of the pews, the funeral caskets of unidentified flood victims. I could see printed cards tacked to each coffin, detailing the sex and description of the enclosed body. For a moment, one of the undertakers' assistants looked directly at me, and I heard him exclaim, "Are you all right?" Then I fainted.

When I came to, I found myself gazing up at my father and a very worried cleric of the church. I was lying on the cool floor of the entranceway where I had stood before I fainted. My father helped me sit up, and the cleric handed me a glass of water, which I took with shaking hands. When I had drunk my fill and reassured the men that I was feeling better, I described for them what I had seen and heard that afternoon.

The cleric nodded his head a few times, unsurprised.

"Yes, yes. Several people have had similar visions of this place," he said when I concluded, "though none was as intense as yours. Usually it is just a quick glimpse of the coffins or the sound of voices. This is a place with a tragic history."

As soon as I felt well enough to stand, we thanked the cleric and hurried from the church. Stopping outside for a moment, I candidly told my father that I didn't want to go anywhere near the Old Stone Bridge with its 40-foot-high pile of debris and its fire and its tortured victims. He agreed and took me to the car. It was only when we left the boundaries of Johnstown that the chill in the air and the murmur of sad voices ceased to haunt me. I gasped with relief and leaned back against my seat.

My father gave me a sharp sideways glance and then looked back at the road. "You know, Patty, I'm a bit disappointed," he said.

My heart sank, and I hastened to apologize to my history-loving father. "I know, Dad. I'm sorry you didn't get to see the Old Stone Bridge or the Johnstown Incline. I could have waited for you in the car."

"Oh no, that's not why I'm disappointed," my father said, surprising me. "I'm just disappointed that now I am the only nonpsychic member in this family. You were the last holdout. Now I'm all alone in a family of crazy people!"

Startled, I burst out laughing and felt the warmth coming back to my cheeks as I giggled and choked and gasped for breath.

"That's better," my father said with satisfaction. "You had me worried back there."

"You and me both," I said fervently. "I think I'd better steer clear of tragic historical sites for the time being."

My father agreed. "But at least your mother will be happy," he added, and I laughed again as we turned onto the highway, leaving the sad ghosts of the Johnstown flood far behind.

The White Lady

ALTOONA

It was dark when he left the office that night, but the moon was full and shone so brightly it dimmed the stars in the late autumn sky. He drew a deep breath of crisp air and stretched his arms out wide to get the kinks out of his back. The project he had been working on was brutal, but tonight it was finally complete, and he could relax.

He hummed softly to himself as he got into the car. It was a perfect night for a drive, and traffic was light, so he decided to take the long way home, over Wopsononock Mountain. There once was a famous hotel and lookout on top of the mountain, but it had burned down in the early part of the twentieth century and was never replaced. The "Wopsy Lookout" was now the haven of television and radio towers. It was also known as the local lovers' lane, he remembered with a grin. There were a few times in the not-so-distant past when he himself had gone parking there with the lady who was now his wife. Good times. Good times!

He turned onto the road leading up the mountain, driving swiftly but carefully. It was a treacherous, winding road, and one particular curve had earned the nickname "Devil's Elbow" because of the many accidents that had occurred there through the years. It was late in the evening, and traffic was sparse. He hadn't seen another car since he'd turned onto the Juniata Gap Road, but now a light appeared ahead of him. It was not bright enough or moving fast enough to be the headlights of another vehicle. Perhaps, he mused, it was the flashlight of a stranded traveler.

He slowed the car a bit, watching as the flickering light drew closer. About a hundred yards ahead, he saw the slight figure of a woman dressed in a tattered white gown, walking along the side of the road. She was carrying an old-fashioned lantern, which was the source of the light he had seen, and was gazing around her with a look of such frantic worry that he pulled the car to the side of the road and rolled down his window.

"Excuse me, miss," he called to the woman in white. "Do you need help?"

The woman turned sharply and gazed at him, hope flashing in her fathomless dark eyes. But when the lantern light fell on his face, her shoulders sagged disappointedly, and she sighed. He wondered who she was looking for so frantically. He asked again: "Do you need help?"

After considering him for a long moment, she nodded and said, "Yes, please. I need a ride to the lookout at the top of the mountain."

He motioned to the car, and she got into the backseat. When he heard the door close, he put the car in gear and started up the mountain. He glanced into the rearview mirror at the woman and then gasped softly, for she wasn't there. He whipped his head

THE WHITE LADY

around quickly and saw her sitting in the seat behind him, her lantern resting beside her. He gave her a puzzled smile and turned his gaze back to the road ahead of him.

"Are you looking for someone?" he asked casually, trying to catch another glimpse of her in the rearview mirror. "Did your car break down somewhere?"

The mirror was empty of all save the darkness of the road behind him and the red glow of his taillights. He could not see the woman in the backseat at all. He risked another glance over his shoulder and saw her sitting behind him. Her face crumpled a little, and she held a lace handkerchief to her eyes, which brimmed with tears.

"I am searching for my husband," she whispered softly. "I know he must be here."

"Were you in an accident?" he asked, forcing his attention back to the treacherous, dark road up the mountain. "Is he still with the car? Perhaps he got a tow somewhere."

They were nearing the Devil's Elbow, and he didn't dare turn around again until they were past the dangerous turn. He risked another glance into the rearview mirror, and again he saw no sign of his passenger. He swallowed convulsively, completely spooked by this encounter. Behind him, the woman in white said, "I have looked everywhere for him. I know he must be here."

He slowed the car as he approached the bend in the road. Suddenly, he heard the sharp, frightened whinny of a horse, followed by the thunder of hooves and the rattle and screech of a carriage that was out of control. The sound came from somewhere on the road ahead of him, and he braked reflexively to avoid an accident. Behind him, the white lady screamed. He glanced over his shoulder and saw the woman's slender body burst into a million tiny sparkles of light. Then the white lady and her lantern disappeared.

He gave a startled shout as his car shuddered to a halt just ahead of the bend called the Devil's Elbow. It was a dangerous place to stop. At any moment, a car could come careening around the corner and hit him. He looked around cautiously for the horse and carriage he had heard a few moments ago. Nothing was there. Slowly, he put his foot on the gas pedal and drove at a snail's pace around the bend. The road on the far side of the bend was empty.

He picked up speed as soon as he was sure it was safe and made record time driving up and over the mountain. His body shook the whole way home.

He sat for several minutes in the darkness of his garage, leaning his face against the wheel of the car and breathing heavily. Dear God, he had seen a ghost. A ghost! What else could it have been? He stayed so long in the garage that his wife came out to look for him. Seeing him sitting so still in the car, she got into the passenger's seat and asked him what was wrong.

Still trembling with fear, he told her about the white lady he had tried to help on the way home. He was afraid his wife wouldn't believe his story, but it burned inside him and needed to be told. To his relief, she started nodding her head, and when he had finished, she said gravely, "It must have been the White Lady of Wopsononock."

"The White Lady?" he asked, feeling a glimmer of recognition when he heard the name.

"She's the ghost of a woman who was killed at the Devil's

Elbow," his wife said. "According to the stories I've heard, the White Lady and her brand-new husband were traveling to the Wopsononock Hotel at the top of the mountain, where they were going to spend the first night of their honeymoon. As they approached the bend in the road that we call the Devil's Elbow, the horse was spooked by the sound of a wild animal, and it bolted, carrying the carriage and its occupants over the edge of the cliff. Both husband and wife were killed in the accident, but the husband's body was never found. From that day to this, the ghost of the White Lady still searches the mountain for her missing husband."

"She kept saying that she was searching for her husband," he said slowly, nodding thoughtfully. "Yes, I think you're right. It must have been the White Lady I saw. And I heard the sound of a carriage accident just before she disappeared."

He felt a little better knowing who his mysterious passenger was and why he hadn't been able to see her in his rearview mirror. He gave his wife a hug and kiss, grateful to have a spouse who believed him even when he came home with such a fantastic story.

"I tell you what," he said as they got out of the car. "That's the last time I'm driving up Wopsononock Mountain at night!"

"I don't blame you a bit," his wife agreed with a chuckle. Taking his hand, she led him into the light and warmth of their kitchen.

13

The Miner-Minstrel

WILKES-BARRE

I spent fifty years down in the mines before my strength gave out and my hands got too crippled with arthritis to work. I was proud of that accomplishment. Not many men live to old age working in a coal mine.

I've lived my whole life in a "mine patch"—that's what we miners called our mining communities. The communities and all the folks in them were owned by the coal companies, body and soul. I was brought into the world by a company doctor, and when I go out of it someday, I'll be buried in a company cemetery. Churches, stores, and schools are all owned by the Coal King—that's what we call our absentee owner. I know one fellow who had the following epitaph carved on his tombstone: "Forty years with pick and drill / Down in the coal to pay my bills. / The Coal King's slave, by now I've passed / Hallelujah, I'm free at last!"

When I was a child, everyone living and working in the mine patches came from Scotland or Wales. Things changed, sometime around 1880, and the patches filled up with miners from all over the world. Suddenly, we were working side by side with Slavs,

Germans, Hungarians, Italians, and some ex-slaves whose ancestors came from Africa. It was an odd mix of folks, and it took a while for things to settle down in the patches. There was a lot of fighting and tension, but as our supervisor used to say, "The coal you dig ain't Slav or Pole or Irish coal. It's just coal." And he was right.

The one thing that made life bearable for us all was music. We were surrounded by song and poetry all day long. Mine workers sang in the branch entries deep below the ground while waiting for the dust and smoke to settle in their "rooms" after they blasted down the coal. Mule drivers sang and joked during the long rides through the mine. Song followed song at the barroom on payday,; sometimes the families of the miners would gather under a moonlit sky with the tower colliery building and culm banks in the background, and we would sing and tell stories, and dance the night away to the smell of coal dust and brimstone. We'd pull out a plate of sheet iron borrowed from the colliery and use it for a dance floor as a fiddler scraped out tune after lively tune. Irishmen would dance with Italian women, and Slav miners mixed with Poles, forgetting their differences for a time.

There were some men among us who were born minstrels, lads who could dramatize a song with the lift of an eyebrow or the gesture of one hand. These men were the soul of the mining patch. They came and went in the manner of the bards of old, traveling to and fro among the patches in the county. Those whose feet were too restless would walk over the whole of anthracite coal country, singing for their meals and bringing delight to all the coal men and their families.

THE MINER-MINSTREL

I was a young man when I first met Nathaniel Kramer, who was a fiddler and a minstrel and a pretty good blacksmith when he set his mind that way. Nat had a voice that was so sweet it could charm the birds, and a manner that was so funny that he had the most hard-core miner rolling on the floor with tears streaming down his cheeks. A whole bunch of us were sitting on the porch of the company store one day when Nat came strolling up the road with his fiddle. He set his case down on the ground, put his fiddle under his chin, and started to sing: "Winter or the summertime / Whether rain or whether shine / Every man is there in line / Seated on the step." He gestured to us with his bow, and we laughed aloud, because there we all were, sitting on the steps of the porch, like always. We liked this new minstrel at once and settle back to wait for more.

Seeing the bright expectation in our faces, Nat scraped away at the fiddle again and sang a sly song about Neddy Kearn's brand-new shovel that was broken by Barney Gallagher down in the coal mine. Well, the fistfight that followed this minor tragedy was tremendous! The other miners gathered 'round to cheer the combatants on, and Neddy Kearn had just about clobbered poor old Barney Gallagher when the mine boss came in and broke up the fight. Nat finished with a wink and a shake of his head, all that fuss and bother "was all about the shovel that was broke in two!" To a man, we rose to our feet on the steps of the company porch and applauded until our hands were sore.

That was the beginning of a lifelong friendship between me and Nat Kramer. He fiddled at my wedding to Cynthia O'Malley, the prettiest girl who ever lived in a mine patch, and he sang special ballads at the christenings of our three daughters and two sons. In return, we always kept a place by the fire for Nat and a warm room for him to sleep in whenever he came to town.

Sometimes, Nat would slip in late at night after we had all gone to bed. Whenever we heard him arrive, the whole family would creep from our beds, gather around the kitchen fireplace, and listen to him fiddle until the dawn. On those nights, Nat would sing to us about the life of the coal miner—about our life—the only life we had ever known.

My hands are horny, hard, and black from working in the vein,
Like the clothes upon my back, my speech is rough and plain;
And if I stumble with my tongue I've one excuse to say,
It's not the collier's heart that's bad, it's his head that goes astray.

(Chorus)

> *Down in a coal mine, underneath the ground,*
> *Where a gleam of sunshine never can be found;*
> *Digging dusky diamonds all the year around,*
> *Away down in a coal mine, underneath the ground.*

At every shift, be it soon or late, I haste my bread to earn,
And anxiously my kindred wait and watch for my return;
For death that levels all alike, whate'er their rank may be,
Amid the fire and damp may strike and fling his darts at me.

There came a day when an explosion trapped me and some of the lads in a shaft for a night and a day. The air was going bad, and I thought it was the end for me. I wasn't afraid for myself; there was no pain. Death would be like falling asleep, with heaven on the other side. But I hated to leave Cynthia and the children with so little. I was nearly asleep when a bright light pierced my eyelids. I looked up into the faces of the mine boss and my old friend Nat, who had come down into the mine to help dig me out. I gulped desperate, deep breaths of the clean air and cried like a baby as they pulled me and the other men out of the shaft and into blessed freedom and life.

We were the lucky ones. Only a few decades ago, there was a fire in the Avondale mine that caused a major tragedy. Nat must have read my mind, because he gave me a broad smile and started softly humming the tune of the Avondale Mine Disaster: "A hundred and ten of brave strong men were smothered underground; / They're in their graves till the last day, their widows may bewail / And the orphans' cries they rend the skies all around through Avondale." But there was no disaster on this day. There was only light, and laughter, and within an hour the feel of my wife's arms around me, holding me tight.

Fifty years came and went in a flash, and one special night I found myself sitting in a chair of honor out in the old field under a moonlit sky with the tower colliery building and culm banks in the background. It was my birthday and the day I retired permanently from the coal mine. With me were my loving family: my coal-mining sons and my beautiful daughters, my wonderful grandchildren, and a great-gran or two as well. One or two old friends had survived the mines and were sitting at the head table with me on this great day, and many of the new friends I had made over the years were there as well, celebrating my good fortune.

The youngsters were already dancing to the smell of coal dust and brimstone on the plate of sheet iron we'd borrowed from the colliery as several fiddlers and guitar players scraped out a merry tune, singing ballad after ballad. It was a time to rejoice. A coal miner had made it out of the mine with his life intact and—more rare even than this—some money in his pocket to retire on. Cynthia sat next to me, holding my hand tight and smiling through her tears.

I kept looking around for one face in particular. Finally, I leaned over to Cynthia and asked, "Where's Nat?"

Cynthia looked troubled. "I sent the word out a month ago that we wanted him to come and play at your birthday/retirement party," she said. "You know how hard he is to track down when he is wandering. I'm sure he will be here. He wouldn't let anything stand in the way of his attending your party."

I nodded my head. What she said was true. Nat would come to the party.

It was very late when the impromptu band stopped playing and a voice rang out over the crowd.

"A happy birthday to you, Terry Jenkins, and congratulations on your retirement!"

Nat stood at the head of the iron dance floor with a glass of beer in his hand. The crowd echoed his words and drank a toast to my health. I stood and bowed low in response to the toast, while around me all my family and friends applauded and cheered. Then Nat took out his fiddle and began to play "The Old Miner's Refrain" for me.

I'm getting old and feeble and I cannot work no more,
I have laid my rusty mining tools away;
For forty years and over I have toiled about the mines,
But now I'm getting feeble, old, and gray.
I started in the breaker and went back to it again,
But now my work is finished for all time;
The only place that's left me is the almshouse for a home,
Where I'm going to lay this weary head of mine.

(Chorus)
Where are the boys that worked with me in the
*   breakers long ago?*
Many of them now have gone to rest;
Their cares of life are over, and they've left this world of woe,
And their spirits now are roaming with the blest.

When he finished the song, the entire field erupted into applause, and tears were surreptitiously wiped from many eyes. I went over to the dance floor and gave Nat a bear hug, filled with love and gratitude for this old friend of mine. To my surprise, his clothes were damp and smelled of dirt and mildew. Looking closer, I saw that his eyes were red-rimmed, and his face was far too pale for my liking.

"Old friend, you don't look well," I said, as I pulled back from our hug.

Then Nat said something strange: "I had to come back this once, Terry. Just for you. I'll see you on the other side."

With a sad, sweet smile, Nat walked away into the darkness. I watched him go, knowing in my bones that it was the last time I would ever see him. Cynthia must have seen a shadow cross my face, for she came over and took my hand.

"I told you he would come," she whispered to me. "He loves you like a brother."

I nodded sadly, then forced myself to smile as I turned back to the party.

I didn't want to spoil Cynthia's evening, so I waited until the next day to tell her what Nat had said. "He must be sick," Cynthia concluded when I finished my story. "We should try to find him. He should stay here with the family that loves him during his last days."

She got up from the kitchen table with a look of determination and went over to the wall telephone. Cranking the handle a few times, she called the operator and asked to be put through to Scranton, which was always Nat's next stop on his circuit after Wilkes-Barre. Our eldest grandson was living and working in

Scranton at the time, and Nat usually went to stay with him. Joshua and his wife had missed my birthday party last night because their new baby was ill, so Cynthia had to give him a full update on the party before she could bring up Nat Kramer.

I was listening with only half an ear while I whittled a fancy toy horse for my newest great-gran. But I knew my wife's voice well, and I looked up quickly when a note of fear and alarm entered it.

"What?" Cynthia said. "Are you sure? But he was here last night, I swear. Everyone saw him, heard him play! Terry gave him a hug just before he left."

I hurried to my wife's side. "What is it?" I asked, loudly enough so that my grandson could hear my question over the phone. Cynthia covered the receiver with her hand.

"Joshua says that Nat Kramer is dead. He died of pneumonia last week and was buried in the churchyard near their home."

I sat down hard on the nearest chair, remembering the smell of wet dirt and mildew that had clung to Nat's clothes, remembering his pale face and his parting words. Cynthia was remembering them, too.

"Dear God in heaven," she gasped, the phone slipping from her grasp. She sank to the floor, her head between her knees. We could hear our grandson calling out frantically to us over the phone, but neither of us had the strength to answer him. Finally, I drew in a deep breath, took up the phone again, reassured Joshua that we would call him back, and hung up the receiver. Then I sat down on the floor beside my wife of more than forty years and took her hand in mine.

"You were right, Cynthia," I said finally. "Nat didn't let anything stand in the way of his coming to my party. Not even death."

He must have risen out of his grave very early that morning and walked all the way to Wilkes-Barre with his fiddle in order to play me one last song. I leaned my head back against the wall, suddenly overwhelmed by the love that had prompted such devotion to a lifelong friend. I felt tears rolling down my cheeks, and I could do nothing to check them. Cynthia clung to me, laughing and crying and completely spooked by such an uncanny ending to our friendship with Nathaniel Kramer.

"Though it's not really an ending," I told her when I had calmed down again. "Remember what Nat said. He would see me on the other side."

"And so he will." Cynthia spoke confidently, and she gave me a long, loving kiss. "Someday."

14

The Phantom Stagecoach

STRASBURG

My girlfriend and I decided to take a weekend getaway to Lancaster County—her choice, not mine—and booked ourselves into a nice inn in Bird-in-Hand. Not that we spent much time at the inn. No, my girlfriend was a first-class shopper, and she was in her element among the craft stores and markets and outlets and wineries of Amish Country. Each time I settled myself in front of the TV at the inn, eager to watch some sports, in she'd roll with a bunch of brochures and a shopping list the size of Texas. Then off went the TV and out we'd go, to stroll among the handcrafted goods, scented candles, knick-knacks, and wooden furniture that seemed to be a standard part of every store we entered.

I am a patient man, but after two days of shopping, I found myself losing my cool. It was the fourth crowded quilt shop we visited that was the straw that broke this camel's back. I found my face smashed up against the side of a large quilt featuring a simpering girl-child gathering spring flowers in a pretty field with a smiling cow and a cute red barn in the background. What got to me was the fact that the girl was all sunbonnet and no face. *Who had dressed this poor kid?* I wondered. Why was she in a meadow gathering spring flowers instead of in school? Why was the cow smiling? And why was I standing here breathing in the scent of country apple candles and evaluating the merits of a silly picture on a children's quilt?

I stormed to the front of the store, bumping into eager matrons, small children, and bemused males in my haste to collect my girlfriend and exit the building.

"Where are we going?" my girlfriend asked, surreptitiously trying to loosen my grip on her arm as I pulled her along the street to the car.

"Anywhere but here!" I exclaimed, opening the car door, taking her packages from her hand, and helping her into her seat. I flung the bags into the backseat and got in behind the wheel. "I need air and food and someplace with no knickknacks whatsoever!"

"We're in Amish country," my girlfriend said patiently. "Everybody has knickknacks. It's practically mandatory."

"Well, I'll grant you a few knickknacks if you grant me the food and fresh air."

"How about the railroad depot in Strasburg? We can get something to eat on the dining car of the old steam train," she suggested.

I brightened immediately. Railroads and steam trains were something I could appreciate. There was something manly about a big steam engine, with its power and its fire and smoke. My girlfriend pulled out the map and gave me directions to the depot.

Two hours and one train ride later, I found myself strolling hand in hand toward the parking lot with my girlfriend, a bag full of train memorabilia and books on my arm. (Okay, so I did a little shopping, too. At least the knickknacks at the train depot were manly ones!) The sky was filling with dark storm clouds, and a wind was kicking up all around us. Good, I thought. If it rained, my girlfriend might let me go back to the inn and watch some baseball.

"Didn't you love the story the conductor told us about the ghostly train whistle?" my girlfriend asked, giving me a sideways glance. I knew where this was leading.

"Fairytales and hogwash," I said at once. "Children's stories."

She pouted playfully. "Just because you don't believe in ghosts. . . " she began.

I sighed loudly, interrupting her. "Okay, where's the Ghost Tour?"

There had to be some sort of Ghost Tour around here. They seemed to be all the rage in tourist destinations, and my girlfriend insisted on taking every one.

"It's right here in Strasburg," she said eagerly. "We sign up at the little store on the corner of Main Street at the traffic light. The one right opposite the ice cream shop."

Ice cream! Now that was something else I could get into.

"I'll tell you what," I said. "You can sign us up for the Ghost Tour, and I'll get us some ice cream. Deal?"

"Deal!" she said with satisfaction. Looking into her sparkling brown eyes, I realized that I had been had, but I was used to it by now. She was smart as well as pretty, which was why I liked her so much.

I parked the car on a side street and crossed at the light,

heading toward the ice cream shop through the wind and menacing dusk brought on by the approaching thunderstorm. My girlfriend disappeared into the store selling the Ghost Tour tickets just as a loud rumble of thunder announced the imminent arrival of the rain.

There was no line in the ice cream shop, so I quickly purchased two cones and went to take a seat by the window to watch the growing storm and wait for my girlfriend to come out of the store across the street. The air around me was electrified. The hairs on my arms stood on end, and I felt tense with excitement, though there was really nothing in the street to get excited about. The clouds hovered just above the treetops, and a flash of nearby lightning momentarily blinded me.

Outside, I could hear the clop-clop of horses' hooves moving steadily down the main street. Some poor Amish folk were about to get caught out in the rain, I thought, straining my neck a little, trying to get a glimpse of the picturesque sight of the horse and buggy. The sound of hooves grew louder, as if the buggy were speeding up, trying to outrun the storm. It was very close now. Good thing there was a green light, I thought, because they were coming so quickly that they probably wouldn't be able to stop if it turned red.

A huge gust of wind shook the ice cream shop and thrashed through the branches of the trees. Lightning flashed. Thunder rumbled. The static electricity in the air grew so strong that I felt my hair stand on end. Suddenly, down the center of Main Street, an electric blue, semitransparent coach came bursting into existence out of nowhere. It was pulled by glowing horses with wind-whipped manes and lashing tails whose ghostly hooves never

THE PHANTOM STAGECOACH

once touched the ground. Driving them onward was a spectral coachman in the rough garb of a man from the mid-1800s. Through the coach windows I could see the laughing figures of several men in the Civil War uniforms of the Union army.

The phantom stagecoach raced through the light, shot past the windows of the ice cream shop, and thundered down the street and out of my view. Its wheels never once touched the ground. It was immediately followed by sheets and sheets of rain that came pouring down onto the street and the sidewalk and all the shops.

I sat frozen in my chair, my mouth open and my eyes wide with shock. Good lord! I had just seen a ghost! Several ghosts, in fact. I turned and glanced over to the counter to see if any of the staff had seen the phantom carriage, but they were busy cooking and cleaning, and no one as much as glanced in my direction. There were no other customers in the store that I could consult with. I was on my own in this ghostly sighting.

Carefully moving my girlfriend's dripping ice cream into the hand that held my own cone, I rubbed my eyes with my free hand and carefully looked up and down the street through the rain-streaked window. There was nothing there. Not even a car.

Deciding that I was losing my mind, I absently began eating my ice cream cone. A moment later, I saw my girlfriend emerge from the shop across the street into the downpour. She threw her arms over her head to protect her hair—which took a good half hour to arrange each morning—glanced both ways at the empty intersection, then came running across to the ice cream shop. She burst into the door, looking around for me. I waved from my seat by the window and handed her the dripping cone as she took the seat opposite me.

"We'r signed up for the 7 o'clock Ghost Tour," she told me cheerfully, shaking the rain from her clothes and taking a huge bite of ice cream. I winced slightly. Whenever I bit into ice cream, it made my teeth sting and tingle.

"Will they tell us about the Phantom Stagecoach?" I asked, taking another mouthful of my ice cream.

"Probably," she said, rubbing at some melted chocolate that had dripped onto her chin. "According to the story I heard, several Civil War soldiers were coming home on leave when the stagecoach they were riding turned over during a terrible rainstorm, killing everyone on board. Every once in a while, the stagecoach and its phantom passengers will come racing down Main Street here in Strasburg, usually just before a storm."

Then she looked at me with narrowed eyes. "How did you know about the Phantom Stagecoach?"

"It just went past," I said, leaning back casually. "Just before the storm broke. Spectral horses, coachmen, Civil War soldiers, the whole nine yards."

She stared at me, her eyes round. "Very funny. Ha! Ha!"

I grinned at her. "It did. Honest. Scared me half to death. Does it always appear before a thunderstorm?"

It took me a long time to persuade my girlfriend that I had actually seen a ghost. But finally, she gave a happy shriek of amazement and jealousy and hugged me around the neck. "How exciting! That is so awesome!" she exclaimed.

I was pretty excited myself. How many people ever get to see a real phantom? It was the stuff stories were made of.

"You know what this means, don't you?" my girlfriend asked as we threw away our napkins and prepared to exit into the rain-soaked street.

"What?" I asked, holding the door open for her.

"You'll never scoff at ghost stories again!" she said triumphantly. "In fact, you'll have your own story to tell on the Ghost Tour tonight."

Chuckling, I had to agree with her. Boy, did I ever have a story to tell!

15

Axe Murder Hollow

ERIE

When the threatening rain finally came, it swooped down upon the earth in a torrential downpour that eliminated the evening landscape in moments. Lightning flashed, thunder roared, and the wind nearly blew the car off the road. The storm brought darkness early. Even with the high beams on, there was almost no visibility along the road.

"We'd better stop." Susan had to shout the words to be heard over the racket outside. To her surprise, her cute but rather stubborn boyfriend, Ned, nodded his agreement and turned his car toward the side of the road. But when he stepped on the brake, the car started to slide on the slick pavement, and they went right off the road. Susan screamed once, then hung and prayed until the car slid to a halt in the mud at the bottom of a small incline.

Pale and shaking with nerves, Ned quickly turned to check if she was all right. Susan nodded her head, her blond ponytail tickling the back of her neck in a familiar, soothing way. She reached out an equally shaky hand to touch Ned's cheek and smile into his dark eyes reassuringly. Ned relaxed under her touch, then

looked through the rain-soaked windows. The headlights illuminated trees, bushes, mud, dead leaves, and the occasional green
patch of weeds. Ned swore and turned off the engine.

"I'm going to see how bad it is," he told Susan, and went out
into the storm before she could protest. She saw his blurry figure
in the headlights, walking around the front of the car. Then he
disappeared into the darkness. A moment later, he reappeared
and jumped in beside her, soaking wet.

"The car's not badly damaged, but we're wheel-deep in
mud," he said. "I'm going to have to go for help."

Susan swallowed nervously. They had been driving through a
wooded, sparsely populated area. There would be no quick res-
cue here.

"At least wait until the rain stops," Susan said, but Ned just
grinned at her, his dark eyes amused.

"I'm already soaked, Sue," he said, giving her a light kiss on
the mouth. "A little more rain won't kill me."

His face became stern, and he told her to turn off the headlights and lock the doors until he returned. This section of the
road was reputed to be haunted, and he wanted to make sure she
felt comfortable staying alone in the car, where she would be
warm and dry. Susan nodded her agreement. Once the car was
secured to his satisfaction, Ned gave her another kiss, then slid
out into the rain. Susan quickly locked the door behind him and
sat rubbing her hands nervously.

Axe Murder Hollow. Although Ned hadn't said the name
aloud, they both knew what he had been thinking when he told
her to lock the car. There was an old, abandoned farmhouse
somewhere near here, where a man had once taken an axe and

hacked his wife to death in a jealous rage over an alleged affair with a farmhand. Supposedly, the axe-wielding spirit of the husband continued to haunt this section of the road, searching for the man who had stolen the affections of his wife.

Outside the car, Susan heard a muffled shriek, a loud thump, and a strange gurgling noise. She could hear the bushes shaking with more force than the wind could explain. But she could see nothing in the darkness that surrounded the car.

Susan sat bolt upright in fright. "Ned?" she whispered, afraid to call out loud. Then she realized that Ned was probably already far up the road in search of help. Frightened, she shrank down into her seat until her head was below the dashboard. Outside, the rattling, thumping, dragging noises continued for a few moments, and then all was silent save for the rain pounding on the roof of the car. After a few minutes of tense silence, Susan decided that it must have been two raccoons fighting one another.

She sat in silence, growing colder as the heat seeped out of the car. Then she noticed another sound through the harsh wind and rain. Bump. Bump. Bump. It was a soft sound, like something being blown by the wind so that it knocked against something else. She found herself listening for the sound, straining in the direction of the woods, trying to see what was causing the small, steady noise. She could see nothing at all in the darkness.

Suddenly, the car was illuminated by a bright light, and an official sounding voice was telling her to get out of the car. Susan relaxed. Ned must have found a police officer. Trembling with relief, she unlocked the door and stepped out of the car. As her eyes adjusted to the bright light, she unconsciously looked

AXE MURDER HOLLOW

around for the source of the bumping noise. Then she saw it.

Hanging by his feet from the tree next to the car was the dead body of her boyfriend, Ned, displayed like a prize deer that has been taken by a hunter. Her horror-stricken eyes took in his bloody throat, which had been cut so deeply that he was nearly decapitated. His beautiful brown eyes were wide open and frozen into an expression of surprise and fear, which ripped through her gut like a knife. She stood for a moment, frozen with terror. The wind whipped around her cold body and swung her boyfriend's corpse gently back and forth so that it thumped against the tree. Bump. Bump. Bump.

At the sound, Susan screamed and ran desperately toward the official-sounding voice and the light. The figure was standing on the incline just above the car. As she drew close, she realized that light was not coming from a flashlight. Standing there was the glowing, translucent figure of a man with wild hair, maddened eyes, and a tender smile on his face. She could see trees and rain-wet bushes right through his body, but the large axe he held in his hands was solid and most definitely real.

Susan tried to scream, but the sound gurgled and died in her throat. She backed away from the glowing figure until she bumped into the car. Even as her hand fumbled for the door, she knew there was no escape. Where could you hide from an axe-wielding ghost?

"Playing around with the farmhand when my back was turned," the ghost whispered softly, stroking the sharp blade of the axe with his fingers. "You've been very naughty."

The last thing she saw was the glint of the axe blade in the eerie, incandescent light as it swung forward toward her neck.

PART TWO
Powers of Darkness and Light

16

Bloody Mary

HARRISBURG

I finished pounding the nail into the horseshoe and carefully set the horse's hoof down onto the floor. The mare shifted her weight gratefully back onto all four feet and sighed deeply. I patted her flank, then put my tools down and led her into the small stall I kept next to the smithy for the use of my customers. She settled down quickly and began pulling at the hay in the rack.

"Papa," I heard a small voice call from behind me. I turned and smiled when I saw my only daughter, my sweet little Emily. With her cornflower blue eyes and long golden braids, she was the image of her mother. Emily had a deep basket hanging from her little arm. Even from here, I could smell roast chicken and sage-and-onion stuffing. My favorite.

"Mama asked me to bring you lunch, since you have such a busy schedule today," Emily said. She carried the basket into the smithy and set it onto a low table. "She sent extra so I could have lunch with you," she added with a grin that revealed a missing front tooth. I grinned back and bowed her into a chair.

We sat munching the good food and talking about which animals I had seen today and who needed what metalwork done around town. Thump, thump, thump. Emily's small feet bounced against the leg of the chair as we talked together. Suddenly the thumping stopped, and Emily's blue eyes grew large. She was staring out into the yard, and I saw her tremble. I turned at once, wanting to see what had upset her.

An old crone with a cruel, wrinkled face and long, straggly white hair stood in the yard, leaning heavily on a cane. It was Bloody Mary. Or rather, it was Frau Gansmueller, I should have said. Bloody Mary was a nickname the children had given the old woman long ago. They thought she was a witch and were frightened by her.

Frau Gansmueller lived deep in the forest in a tiny cottage and sold herbal remedies for a living. None of the good folk living in town dared to cross the old crone for fear that their cows would go dry, their food stores rot away before winter, their children take sick of fever, or any number of terrible things that an angry witch could do to her neighbors.

I stepped hastily into the yard and sketched a bow to the old woman. "How may I be of service, Frau Gansmueller?" I asked quickly. Bloody Mary glared at me with narrow, coal-black eyes.

"I've come for an andiron, Herr Smith," she said in her soft, sibilant voice. I repressed a shiver at the soft hissing tone. Her voice sounded like that of a talking snake.

"Fine, fine," I stammered. I hurried inside, motioned to Emily to stay where she was, and brought out a new andiron for the old crone. I handed it to her, naming a sum half of what it was worth. I wasn't taking any chances on upsetting the old witch. She examined it critically before putting it into her basket next to the small mirror she always carried. The she counted out the money into my hand.

As she turned to leave, Bloody Mary stopped suddenly, glancing back into the smithy. "What a pretty little girl you have, Herr Smith," she said, offering Emily a crooked smile and stroking the small mirror in her basket. Emily turned white with fear and smiled back.

"Thank you, Frau Gansmueller," I said as politely as I could. She hobbled away then, and I watched her until she disappeared around a bend in the road. A moment later, a small hand crept into mine, and Emily said, "I do not like her, Papa."

"Neither do I, child," I said. Then a stab of fear went through my heart. What would Bloody Mary do to Emily if she ever heard the child saying such things about her? I added, "But we must always be polite to her, Emily, and never speak unkindly about her. Promise me that you will always be polite and kind."

Emily looked deeply into my eyes and nodded solemnly. "I promise, Papa," she said, and I knew she would keep her word. We finished our meal in silence, then Emily took the basket home to her mama.

It was about a week after the incident at the smithy that the first little girl went missing from our town. Little Rosa, the daughter of the shoemaker, disappeared from her home in the middle of the night. She was just a wee mite of a girl who rarely ever left her yard. A search party was formed. We scoured the woods, the local buildings, and all the houses and barns, but there was no sign of the missing girl. Her mother sat and rocked in a corner all day, clutching her daughter's favorite doll and saying nothing. No one could comfort her.

Then the buxom twelve-year-old daughter of Franklin Taylor went for a walk in the woods with a few friends and did not come home. Her girlfriends looked everywhere but could not find her. Another search party was formed, and we examined every tree, every meadow, every stream, to no avail. A few brave souls even went to Bloody Mary's cottage in the woods to see if the witch had taken the girl, but she denied any knowledge of the disappearance.

Next it was Theresa, the brown-eyed, eight-year-old daughter of the basketmaker who went to fetch groceries from the mercantile and did not return. Again we searched, and again the girl remained missing. Everyone in town was frantic with fear. The young girls were instructed to walk in pairs and never to go out without letting their parents know about it. Of course, Bloody Mary was at the back of everyone's mind. Who else but a witch could make three young girls disappear so completely? But there was no proof, and no one dared to say anything.

During the hunt for young Theresa, Bloody Mary had insisted that the girl's father come into her house and search it, so that no suspicion should attach itself to her. The cottage was completely normal save for a fancy mirror on the kitchen wall next to the fireplace, a strange luxury for a poor woman's house. Stranger still was the way the mirror sometimes reflected things that weren't there. The basketmaker glimpsed his house in the village within the glass as he turned away from his examination of the fireplace chimney, but when he walked over to look in the mirror, it reflected only his face and the room behind it. Not surprisingly, the basketmaker found nothing else in the cottage or grounds of Bloody Mary to connect her with his daughter's disappearance.

My wife was keeping Emily in the house all the time now. Only the boys went to the schoolhouse each day, while my wife tutored Emily at home. Sometimes, as I worked at the lathe or hammered hot horseshoes, I remembered Bloody Mary looking into the smithy at Emily and telling me what a pretty child she was. In those moments, I would shiver uncontrollably, unable to warm myself in spite of the heat pouring off the hot smithy fire.

"Herr Smith," a sibilant voice calling from the smithy doorway broke into my thoughts. I knew that voice. It was Bloody Mary. I turned to look at the crone and bit my lip to keep from exclaiming aloud in amazement. Her haggard appearance had changed dramatically. She looked younger and much more attractive.

"How may I be of service, Frau Gansmueller?" I asked, laying down my hammer and tongs.

"I need some new pothooks," Bloody Mary said, her black eyes snapping at me with a malicious amusement that made my hands shake with fear. I drew in a deep breath before I fetched some pothooks for her. Again, I named a low price, and again she examined them carefully before paying me.

"Say good day from me to your mistress and your pretty young daughter," Bloody Mary said, fingering the mirror in her basket thoughtfully. Then she gave me a wicked smile and turned away with a rather flirtatious flick of her long skirts. I swallowed hard as I watched her leave. Her reference to Emily frightened me badly.

As soon as I could, I closed the shop and hurried home. To

BLOODY MARY

my relief, I found Emily studying her books in the corner, her blond head bent industriously over her work. My wife looked up from her cooking in surprise at my early arrival. I took her aside and told her about Bloody Mary's visit. She gasped, and her body started trembling uncontrollably. I took her into my arms, and we clung together for a long time. Then we discussed the matter and decided that the child would have to go and stay with her grandmother until the crisis had passed. Until arrangements could be made, one of us would have to be with her at every moment of the day. With this decided, we went and broke the news to Emily and her brothers.

I lay awake late into the night, praying for the safety of my little girl. I had barely dozed off before I was awakened by my wife. She had a sore tooth and was finding it hard to lie on her right side. She motioned me back to sleep and went downstairs to find the herbal remedy given to her by the apothecary.

I was awakened for the second time by soft strains of music that seemed to be coming from everywhere and nowhere at the same time. Even as I listened, the eerie, luring melody faded away. And then I heard my wife screaming.

I jumped out of bed and ran downstairs. My wife was racing out the front door, her blue eyes fixed on a small, barefooted figure clad in a white nightdress that was walking toward the edge of town. It was Emily! I leaped passed my wife and ran to intercept my daughter. Emily was in a trance, a happy smile on her face, her eyes glazed. She must be hearing the same music that had awakened me.

I caught her in my arms, but she pulled away immediately and continued walking toward the edge of town and the dark woods beyond. I was shocked. Emily was a tiny girl, but she had thrust my work-hardened blacksmith's body away as if I were a stripling. I ran forward and grabbed hold of her again, bracing my body as she struggled against me. My wife wrapped her arms around my waist, holding on tightly and screaming for help.

Her desperate cries woke our neighbors, and they came to assist us in our struggle. Lights went on everywhere as the towns-folk realized that another child was in trouble. Suddenly, a sharp-eyed lad gave a shout and pointed toward a strange light at the edge of the woods.

Leaving my wife and the other women to restrain Emily, I led the men toward the mysterious light. As we entered the field just outside the woods, we saw Bloody Mary standing beside a large oak tree, holding her small mirror in one hand and a magic wand in the other. The wand was pointed toward my house, and reflected in the mirror was the beautiful young face of my daughter. Bloody Mary was glowing with an unearthly radiance as she set her evil spell upon Emily.

Many of the men who had responded to my wife's screams had the forethought to bring guns and pitchforks. One of them thrust a gun into my hand as we ran toward the witch. "It has silver bullets," he shouted to me. I nodded grimly. Silver bullets were the only kind that could kill a witch.

When she heard the commotion, Bloody Mary broke off her spell and fled back into the woods. I stopped, took aim with the gun, and shot at her. The bullet hit Bloody Mary in the hip, and she fell to the ground. Immediately, angry townsmen swarmed upon her, pulling her to her feet and carrying her back into the field. Grimly, I picked up the wand and the mirror that had fallen into the dirt and leaves when I shot their owner.

The judge, who had been the first neighbor to arrive on the scene when we tried to restrain the entranced Emily, quickly pronounced Bloody Mary guilty of witchcraft, kidnapping, and the murder of the three missing girls. He sentenced her to death at the stake, and the townsmen immediately built a huge bonfire, right there in the field. They tied the witch and her magic wand to the wood and set it ablaze. I smashed the magic hand mirror myself.

As she burned, Bloody Mary glared at us through the flames. Staring straight into my eyes, she screamed a curse against all of us. "If anyone," she cried, "mentions my name aloud before a mirror, I will send my spirit to them and will revenge myself upon them in payment for my death!" The witch pointed her hand toward the shards of glass at my feet as she spoke. For a moment they glowed blue, then faded again into darkness.

Many who heard the curse shuddered and stepped back from the fire, but I stood as still as stone and watched as the evil woman paid for her black deeds. When she was dead, I led the villagers to her house in the woods, where we smashed her other magic mirror. With the destruction of the mirror, the concealment spell on the cottage lifted, and we soon found the unmarked graves of the little girls the evil witch had murdered and buried underneath the woodpile. According to the records she kept, she had created a spell that used their blood to make her young again.

So the lives of the other young girls in town were spared, and my Emily was safe at last. My daughter grew into a beautiful young woman who married the minister's son and had three children of her own. But Bloody Mary's curse also lived, if only in rumor. Tales have been told of young people who were foolish enough to chant Bloody Mary's name before a darkened mirror, and so summoned the vengeful spirit of the witch. It is said that the witch tore the poor victims' bodies to pieces and ripped their souls from their mutilated flesh, trapping them forever in burning torment inside the mirror with her. Having seen the witch at work, I find I cannot discount the tales, though I myself have never tried it.

17

Room for One More

PHILADELPHIA

Peter came to the city for a job interview, but he elected to spend the night at the home of friends in a nearby suburb rather than in a hotel. He hadn't seen his friends in several years, so there was much to talk about. They lingered over dinner and then sat around the fireplace with drinks and dessert until after midnight.

By all rights, Peter should have fallen asleep as soon as his head hit the pillow, but for some reason, he tossed and turned and dozed, only to waken with a start. He was nervous, but it had nothing to do with the upcoming interview. What he felt was a much deeper dread, like that of a condemned person awaiting the approaching dawn when the hangman would come for him.

Finally, Peter fell into a light sleep and started to dream. He was wide awake and restless in his dream, and his dream self rose and went over to the open window. A light summer breeze blew in through the screen, and he could smell the roses that climbed the trellis on the side of his friends' house.

In the street below, bright headlights appeared. A large black hearse drew up in front of the house and parked under a street-lamp. Inside the hearse was crammed with people. The driver got out and looked up at the window where Peter stood. The driver's face was a twisted, hideous mask with black-rimmed eyes that glowed red in the darkness.

"Come down," the driver called up at him. "There's room for one more," the driver said with an evil leer that struck terror into Peter's heart. He gestured toward the back of the hearse.

"No, thank you," Peter croaked, his throat suddenly dry, and backed away from the window.

Peter held his breath as the twisted form of the driver stood silently at the side of the road for one minute, then two. Finally, the driver got back into the hearse and drove away. When the gleam of the taillights disappeared into the distance, Peter gasped for breath, his heart pounding so hard that it hurt. Then he woke from his dream and lay sweating under the covers. The smell of roses filled the room, but their scent no longer delighted him. It reminded him too much of the bouquets he sometimes saw at funeral parlors or adorning gravestones.

His friends commented upon his haggard appearance the next morning, and Peter told them about his dream. "It seemed so real," he concluded. His friends chuckled and told him that he was just jittery about his upcoming interview. Reluctantly, he agreed with them and shook off the fear.

Peter arrived in the city a little before noon and made his way to the towering office building where the interview was to take place. He met with several different managers during the course of the next few hours, and his interviews went very well. He was sure that he would get a job offer within the week.

Peter was humming as he left the office and made his way

toward the elevator. Suddenly, the scent of roses wafted through the air, and he stopped dead, staring at a vase full of beautiful flowers that was sitting on a small table beside the elevator. The floral arrangement reminded him of the bouquets he had seen placed beside gravestones in his local cemetery.

In front of him, the elevator bell chimed, and the doors slid open. The elevator was crammed full of people. Peter counted eight men and women already in the small interior and hesitated, unsure whether to enter it or wait for the next one. For some reason, his glance drifted sideways toward the roses. Then a voice from the rear of the elevator called: "Come in. There's room for one more."

Peter looked up sharply, startled by the words, which echoed those from his nightmare. His eyes met those of a tall man with a twisted, hideous mask of a face who was standing at the back of the elevator. The man's black-rimmed eyes had a faint, red glow where the pupils should be. Peter recognized the man at once: It was the driver of the hearse from his dream.

"No, thank you," Peter whispered, as the overpowering smell of roses filled his senses.

After a moment, the elevator doors slid shut, and it began chiming its way downward. Suddenly, there was the metallic twang of a cable snapping, then the roar of an out-of-control elevator as it plunged down the shaft. The screaming of the passengers was cut off abruptly by the sound of a massive crash. There were a few follow-up rumbles, then all the sounds ceased.

For a moment, Peter stood frozen in horror; then he ran for the staircase and raced down the many flights to the ground floor to see if he could help. The lobby was filled with emer-

ROOM FOR ONE MORE

gency personnel by the time he reached it, but it was obviously too late for the people in the elevator.

Seven bodies were pulled from the wreckage. Peter kept insisting to the rescuers that he had seen eight people in the elevator just before it crashed, but the body of the hearse driver was never found.

Hexed!

READING

When Ike Yoder first came to Reading, he bought himself a rundown old farm just outside town and moved onto the 163-acre property with his plump wife and his eleven children. The family worked hard from sunup to sundown, tending the farm chores, going to church, contributing to the community. Within ten years, the farm was all paid off, the buildings were in prime condition, and the Yoder family was making a prosperous living. Life was very good.

Then a mysterious illness fell upon Ike Yoder. Day after day, he would faithfully do his work, attend the local town meetings, and act as a church deacon. But he grew thin and pale, and folks soon noticed that he moved slowly, like an old man. The Yoder family was alarmed. Mrs. Yoder pressed food and drink upon her husband at every occasion, and he ate with the appetite of a young boy, but he did not gain any weight.

The local doctor was brought in to examine Ike. The doctor prescribed a treatment of castor oil and herbal remedies, but none of the medicines worked. So the Yoder family sent for specialists from the nearby cities. These expensive physicians poked and prodded poor Ike and gave him strange medications that tasted awful and made him feel even sicker than before. Nothing helped. Ike continued to lose weight, becoming so pale and listless that Mrs. Yoder was afraid she would lose him altogether. The Yoder sons and daughters fretted and moped and tended to their chores with a listlessness that almost equaled that of their father, so great was their distress.

One by one, the specialists all told Ike that there was nothing more they could do. It would be best if he put his affairs in order and wrote his will. Well, Ike might be weary and thin, but he wasn't ready to die! He talked things over with Mrs. Yoder, who suggested that they call in the local hex doctor. Ike knew then how very frightened his wife was for him, for she did not approve of powwowing, a type of folk medicine that included faith healing and occult practices. But they had both observed the powwow doctor getting results when all hope was lost, and so Ike agreed to see him.

The hex doctor was a mysterious figure who was quietly important in their community. The powwow man was reputed to have special knowledge and magical power. It was rumored that he possessed the *Sixth and Seventh Books of Moses*, the tome from which he had learned the secrets of the great prophet himself, including the magical marks, seals, amulets, and symbols to protect against evil and drive it away. His collection also included the book *Egyptian Secrets, or White and Black Art for Man and Beast* by Albertus Magnus. This book was centuries old, and within it were suggested techniques for curing sickness, for obtaining holding powers over other people, and for many other fearful things.

The hex doctor was tall and very thin, with a shock of unruly white hair, a sharp-cornered face, a soft voice, and snapping black eyes. The first thing he did was to question the patient about his symptoms. Then he made Ike lie down on the bed, and he waved his hands rhythmically above the farmer's prone figure, chanting softly all the while. Afterward, the hex doctor allowed Ike to sit up, as he inquired of him: "Do you have any enemies?"

"None, sir," Ike Yoder replied. The hex doctor looked to Mrs. Yoder, who shook her head. "None that I know of," she said.

The hex doctor frowned in thought. "All the signs point to a hex of some sort," he said. "Perhaps you have an unknown enemy." He fetched a book from his pack. The Yoders recognized it at once. It was *Der lang verborgene Schatz und Haus Freund,* known in English as *The Long Lost Friend* by John George Hohman. It contained a collection of supernatural recipes, spells, and procedures for the occult healer. The Yoders exchanged uneasy glances as the hex doctor consulted the text, looking up the words for some powerful, powwowing incantation. The item was swiftly located, and the hex doctor put himself in a trance in the hopes of discovering the identity of the Yoders' enemy.

"I see. . . " the hex doctor began in a deep, booming voice quite unlike his natural one, "I see an old man. He is dressed in blue trousers with thin white stripes. He has a small beard on his chin and a hand that shakes with palsy. Over his arm, he carries a red horse blanket."

"That's Jake Wetzel," Mrs. Yoder exclaimed. "He is our neighbor to the south."

The hex doctor blinked several times to bring himself out of his trance. "Does he hold anything against you?" he asked the Yoders.

"He tried to buy my lower field a while back," Ike said slowly, "the one with the stream running through it, but I refused to sell. I don't aim to split up my land."

"Ah," said the hex doctor softly. His eyes seemed to pierce through Ike's skull. "And did Jake say anything to you when you refused to sell?"

"No," Ike said slowly. "He didn't say anything." The way the farmer spoke told the hex doctor that something had occurred to him.

"Did he do anything?" the hex doctor asked, very softly indeed.

"*Ja, ja!*" Mrs. Yoder broke in. "He came to the field every evening just at sundown for a week following his talk with Ike, and he waved his red horse blanket up and down three times, flapping it right over the field as if he owned it. We got so tired of his antics that our eldest son finally chased him away with a shotgun, and that was the last we've seen of him."

"So that is it," said the hex doctor solemnly. "Jake Wetzel hexed you, Ike, because you would not sell your land. You are ferhexed [bewitched] and will die if you do not break the curse."

Mrs. Yoder almost fainted and had to be helped into a chair.

"What must we do?" Ike asked the hex doctor. The hex doctor gave them a series of detailed instructions, of which they took careful note. Then he left the house, and Mrs. Yoder went down to the kitchen to carry out the hex doctor's cure.

First, Mrs. Yoder melted wax and formed it into the figure

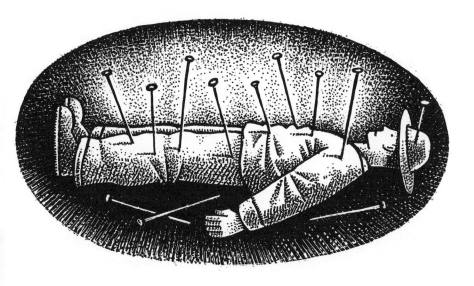

HEXED!

of a man, declaring that the name of the image was Jake Wetzel. This was done to "fix" the image upon the man who had hexed her husband. Then she took out her sewing kit, drew forth her box of pins, and began sticking them one by one into the image, to "torture" it into releasing the hex. Finally, she threw the wax image into the fire to burn, thus destroying the one who had tried to destroy her husband. When the wax image was reduced to a puddle underneath the grate, the cure was complete. Sobbing with weariness and fear, Mrs. Yoder went upstairs to tell her husband that she had carried out the hex doctor's instructions.

Then the waiting began. For seven long days, Ike lay in bed, growing thinner and paler by the day. Mrs. Yoder began to fear that the hex doctor's cure had not worked and that her husband would die. Then, on the seventh day, Jake Wetzel dropped dead right in front of his house. At the same moment, the strength returned to Ike's body, and he sat up, his cheeks flushing with color and his eyes sparkling with renewed health and vigor. "Mother! I am hungry!" he bellowed down the stairs. Mrs. Yoder came running up from the kitchen, her hands covered in flour. She started laughing and crying in delight when she saw her husband, who was already climbing out of bed.

The Yoder children came running into the house soon afterward with the news of Jake Wetzel's death. They found their father consuming large quantities of food at the kitchen table. "Thank God," the oldest son exclaimed. His siblings echoed him, and they all ran to hug their father.

From that day on, Ike Yoder was a healthy man.

19

The Goblin

EASTON

The old mission house had been in ruins long before the French and Indian War began in 1755, and the rumors surrounding it were vile and strange. It had belonged to the Jesuit monks who had come to convert the "heathens" in the new world, but it had been abandoned not long thereafter. It was said that an evil monk-turned-goblin still haunted the place in his rough robes. The goblin was said to sound the chimes of the Angelus, trying to lure people into the mission house so he could destroy them. Several locals claimed to have heard the bells ringing, but the sound faded away whenever a human drew near the ruined mission.

Thus was the state of affairs when a small troop of British soldiers and their captain found themselves trapped outside in a terrible, swirling snowstorm. Seeing shelter nearby, they left the road and took refuge inside the abandoned building. A roaring fire and the leather bottles containing spirits soon had the soldiers laughing and singing merrily. The ruined halls of the mission house soon echoed with profanity and lewd songs of the sort that would cause any good monk to turn over in his grave.

The captain of the troop, after taking a deep swig from a bottle, suddenly shouted: "Bless me, but I recognize this place! It's the haunted mission house that the old farrier told us about when he replaced my horse's shoe."

"Haunted by who?" asked a brawny Scotsman with a broad red mustache.

"An evil old monk," the captain said with a grin. "And a Frenchman to boot! It's a good thing he is roasting down below, lads, or he might come back and destroy us Englishmen for daring to desecrate his mission."

"Tell us the story," urged the Scotsman, leaning back against the wall and moving his boots closer to the fire.

The captain fortified himself with a drink, then told the following tale. There was once a monk at the mission who loved money and power more than he loved God. He would hear the confession of the good folk who attended the mission, then would blackmail them into giving him gold and silver to keep their darkest secrets. He turned many a wayward sinner's feet toward the fires of hell rather than the gates of heaven, encouraging their crimes in secret while he reviled them in public.

It was after he beat one poor old woman to death that the evil monk was imprisoned and sentenced to hang for his crimes. But just after he was cut down from the noose and pronounced dead, his corpse began to transform before the horrified eyes of the people. The face twisted, and small tusks sprang from either side of his nose. His shock of white hair grew long and greasy, and two pointed canines emerged from his slit of a mouth. The goblin-monk opened eyes that glowed yellow even in the light of noonday, and his feet now ended in claws rather than toes. The people screamed and fled, and no prayer of his former brothers-in-faith could banish the goblin. It disappeared into the forest, only to return at night and prey upon the monks of the mission who had been responsible for its death. After five of the brothers had fallen to the goblin, the rest of the monks abandoned the mission and moved to another part of the country. Since that time, the mission house had slowly fallen into ruin.

"They say," the captain continued, leaning forward conspiratorially, "that the goblin still visits the mission on the anniversary of his death. He comes to the door at midnight, his presence heralded by the sound of the chimes of the Angelus. Then a hollow knocking sound is heard. Anyone brave enough to answer the door will find a cowled figure standing there, dressed in the robes of a monk. Those he encounters in the mission will never leave it alive!"

There was a hush following his last words, and a gust of wind rattled the windows of the room. The men jumped in fright, then laughed at themselves. High above the sound of the wind, a faint chiming could be heard.

"Hark to that! Is that the sound of the Angelus?" the Scotsman called out mockingly, holding a hand to his ear.

"It's only the wind, you old fool," shouted the youngest soldier, who was still pale and shivering from the scary story told by the captain.

At that moment, there came a hollow knocking from the front door. Bang! Bang! Bang! All seven men jumped and whirled to face the entryway. Their ears hummed with the sound of their own blood, and they could feel their hearts pounding in terror.

"It's the goblin," the youngest soldier squeaked.

"N . . . nonsense," the captain stammered, trying to ignore his shaking body and clammy hands. "It is probably a hunter who was caught in the storm. Come in!" he bellowed over the roaring of the storm.

The door slammed open. Standing in the entryway was a cowled figure dressed in the robes of a monk. It appeared faceless in the storm-swept darkness. The captain fell back in his chair, his hands gripping the arms until they turned white. His head was swimming with all the alcohol he had consumed, and he couldn't breathe.

The hooded monk strode toward the cowering soldiers, and his hand closed over the top of one of the leather bottles.

"Ha!" the Scotsman said suddenly with a grin. "So you are not a ghost, eh? You're just another poor wayfarer looking for shelter and a drink. Sit by the fire, then, neighbor, and have a drink to the health of our good King George."

"Aye! Drink," the other soldiers shouted, laughing to cover their uneasiness.

The faceless black figure did not respond to their words. It stood silently in front of them, clutching the bottle. As the eerie silence lengthened, the faces of the watching soldiers grew sharp and pale, and the Scotsman ceased to smile. The captain slowly leaned forward, trying to see the face inside the monk's hood, but the figure turned away sharply and walked over to the roaring fire. It upturned the bottle of liquor and poured it into the flames. The liquid turned to steam, which rose from the fire, growing thicker and thicker, and though the bottle was soon empty, the stifling gray steam kept increasing, billowing out from the hearth and filling the room.

THE GOBLIN

Just for a moment, the fire lit the face of the hooded monk, and the captain caught a glimpse of a twisted face with small tusks on either side of the nose, of greasy white hair and two canines that indented a slit of a mouth. For a moment, glowing yellow eyes gazed into his. The captain shrieked in terror and sprang out of his chair. Fighting his way through the heavy steam, he called to his men to follow him as he ran out the still-open door and into the raging winter storm.

He clawed his way through the whipping snow and the thick trees until he reached the road. None of his men had followed him from the mission. The captain felt like a fool for running away, but his whole body shuddered when he thought of the face underneath the cowl, and he ran with renewed strength. He banged upon the door of the first farmhouse he reached and gasped out his story to the kind folks who took him in. They shook their heads gravely when they heard that his men had remained behind, and the farmer got out a lantern and accompanied him back to the mission.

The storm gradually ceased as they walked back along the road, and the wind had died to a whisper by the time they entered the grounds of the abandoned mission house. It was dawn when the farmer and the captain went up the steps and opened the front door. The captain braced himself for the jeers of his men, but when the door swung open, he saw six red-coated bodies lying on the floor. They were all dead.

Morning Star

BEDFORD COUNTY

Gray Wolf was the handsomest of the warriors; tall, broad, and strong, fleet of foot, and a good hunter. Many of the nubile maidens of his tribe had cast their eyes upon him with favor, but as yet he had chosen none of them to be his wife. His mother scolded Gray Wolf about his reluctance to marry, but he only chuckled and told her that he would marry when he found a maiden who suited him. His nonchalance irritated his mother, but Gray Wolf was her only son and she loved him dearly, so she held her peace.

There came a time when the white men, following a great chief named Penn, began settling on the tribal lands. The tribe grew afraid that they would be driven away from the bones of their fathers. The chief of the tribe summoned Gray Wolf, whose fleetness of foot made him a good messenger, and sent him to the neighboring tribes to request their attendance at a council to discuss the matter.

Gray Wolf was gone for four sunsets. On the morning of the fifth day, the warrior staggered into the village, covered with grievous wounds and the bite marks of a large beast of prey.

Gray Wolf was feverish and too ill to speak with any sense. His mother and sisters tended his wounds with the herbs given to them by the medicine man.

When the prayers of his family and the herbs had succeeded in restoring some measure of health to the handsome warrior, Gray Wolf told the council that he had been attacked by a large black cat with glowing eyes the color of the moon. The beast had invaded his campsite one evening shortly after he had gone to sleep and had mauled him, clawing his chest and face and biting his shoulders and arms. Gray Wolf had struggled desperately with the creature, fighting to keep its teeth away from his neck. Finally, his hand had closed over his quiver, and he drew forth an arrow and thrust it into the beast's chest. The cat had howled in pain and had retreated back into the forest, leaving the warrior to bind up his wounds as best he could and stagger back to the village to find help.

Thus went the tale that Gray Wolf told the elders of his tribe. To Running Water, who was his best friend, the warrior confided a slightly different story. When he plunged the arrow into the chest of the beast, it had wailed in the voice of a human woman. Gray Wolf had heard distinct words in her cry as the black cat flung herself away from him and ran back into the forest. It had been Gray Wolf's intention to pursue the beast wherever it fled and to kill it, but he was shaken by her strange voice, and instead he had built up the fire, tended his wounds, and slept. In the morning, Gray Wolf had found a broken necklace on the ground where he had been attacked. The amulet took the form of a sunburst and was made out of beads and human finger bones. It was a horrible thing to look upon. When Gray Wolf showed the amulet to his friend, Running Water shuddered and turned away, refusing to touch such a defiled object.

In the days that followed, Gray Wolf grew restless and dreamy eyed. Though his wounds were closed, the vigor and health he once had did not return. He grew careless of his appearance and spent much of his time alone in the woods and thickets rather than hunting with his friends. Finally, Running Water confronted Gray Wolf and asked him what was happening. Gray Wolf's face lit up with a dreamy, strange delight, and he told his friend that he had fallen in love at last. Something about Gray Wolf's statement worried Running Water. He had not seen his friend with any of the village maidens, and there were no other villages nearby.

Running Water carefully inquired about the maiden he had chosen, and Gray Wolf launched into a paean of delight regarding her beautiful skin, her glowing eyes, her long dark hair, her luscious mouth. Her name was Morning Star, and she lived alone in the woods because her family had all been killed by the white men. While hunting one early morning, Gray Wolf had seen her on her way to the stream to bathe. Although he should have turned his eyes away from her unclothed form, Gray Wolf had been transfixed by her beauty. He had followed her and spoken to her while she bathed. She had been annoyed by his presence at first, but Gray Wolf had appeased her with the offering of several rabbits, and at last she had allowed him to know her. He had visited her every day since then, and his heart was sick with love for his Morning Star.

Running Water studied his friend intently. Gray Wolf did indeed look heart-sick. He was pale and wan, and the muscles of his body were losing their tone. His hair had come loose from its bindings and was in disarray. Running Water was afraid of this Morning Star. If she were a normal maiden, surely she would have sought out another village after her family had perished. A maiden alone had no protection and would not last long among the dangers of the forest, especially when winter came.

Lightly, so as not to offend his friend, Running Water suggested that he might try sleeping a little more and seeing a little less of his beloved Morning Star, else he was likely to die of love sickness. Gray Wolf's face clouded, and he shook his head. "I cannot sleep," he told Running Water. "Every night, I dream of the black cat. It comes to me, licks open my wounds, and drinks my blood." He rubbed his throat unconsciously, and his hair swung back, revealing two swollen marks where the black cat's teeth had bitten him.

Running Water felt his heart begin to pound within him. He was filled with apprehension and fear for his friend. Remembering Gray Wolf's story of the black cat with a woman's voice, and the evil necklace of human finger bones Gray Wolf had found at the place where he was attacked, Running Water was sure that Morning Star and the black cat were one and the same entity. Running Water urged his friend to bring the maiden to live in the village with him, or else to forsake her and look to his own health instead. His words angered Gray Wolf, and they parted bitterly.

Still, Running Water was concerned for his friend. He spent the next night in the woods outside Gray Wolf's home, waiting and watching. At length, he heard the soft padding of large feet, and a huge black cat slunk into the village and crept into the home of the warrior. It cried out in a voice that was neither that

MORNING STAR

of beast nor woman, and Running Water expected the village to rouse at the terrible sound, but an uncanny stillness lay over everything, and no one stirred.

Then Gray Wolf emerged from his shelter, with the black cat twining and purring around him. His eyes were glazed and unfocused as he followed the creature into the woods. Running Water aimed an arrow at the creature, but it kept Gray Wolf's body between itself and Running Water at all times, as if sensing he were near. So Running Water followed them into the woods, keeping knife and bow at hand, seeking a chance to kill the evil thing that had ensorcelled his friend.

The creature led Gray Wolf to a small clearing outside a cave. Then it rose on its hind legs and pawed at the warrior's shirt until the laces came open, revealing the wounds at his throat. Running Water tried to draw an arrow but found to his horror that his body was fixed in one place. Unable to do more than watch, he saw the creature open the wounds with its rough tongue. Then, before his eyes, it transformed into a beautiful, sensuous, unclothed woman who drank the blood of the warrior as Gray Wolf stood transfixed in the clearing before her cave. Such was the look of extreme pain and delight that appeared on Gray Wolf's face that Running Water wanted to cry out, but he could not.

Running Water's eyes remain riveted on the beautiful woman, and he felt desire running through him, terrible and fierce. For a moment, he sensed a little of what his friend must be feeling, and it terrified and entranced him. Then the woman looked straight at him, her mouth covered with blood, and smiled. Her eyes glowed with the color of the moon. They were the eyes of a beast. She had known he was there all along. Turning to Gray Wolf, she struck him in the chest, her arm entering through his flesh as if it were not there. Gray Wolf came out of his trance and stared in horror down at the beautiful, naked woman before him as she ripped out his heart.

"No, Morning Star," Running Water shouted, horror releasing his voice from the creature's spell. "No!"

"It tastes better with the fear," she said, as she held Gray Wolf's still-beating heart in her bloody hand. Before her, Gray Wolf staggered backward and fell dead to the ground. Morning Star turned gloatingly toward Running Water and raised his friend's heart to her lips. Running Water strained desperately against the spell that still bound his body, but it held him transfixed. Then he felt the spell cover him thickly, suffocatingly, as if a blanket were thrust over his mouth and nose. He gasped desperately for breath and fell senseless to the ground.

Running Water awoke to the sound of horrified voices and looked up into the faces of his people. He lay at the very edge of the village, unharmed save for the bloody handprints upon his shirt, and he knew that Morning Star had carried his unconscious body home after her terrible feast.

Running Water stood before the council and told them the whole terrible story. A search was mounted at once, but Morning Star had disappeared, and Gray Wolf's body with her. It was found a moon later, wrapped in elk bark just outside the cave where Morning Star once lived. In his chest was a gaping hole where the heart had been ripped out, but the body was entirely drained of blood. Around his neck was a sunburst necklace made of beads and human finger bones.

Thereafter, the warriors were all instructed to hunt in pairs, and to beware of a black cat with eyes that shone the color of the moon. But Morning Star was not seen again in those parts.

Many years passed, and gradually the story of Morning Star was forgotten as new tales of life and love and death were created within the village. Then one morning, Running Water, who was a venerable old man and very full of years, woke from a deep sleep to find a newly made sunburst necklace made of beads and human finger bones lying mockingly beside him on his sleeping mat.

Morning Star had returned.

21

Dark Cathlin

READING

When Phillip was still a young man, he fell in love with the beautiful dark Cathlin, who was the daughter of a high-class colonel who lived in the nearby town. As a poor farmer, Phillip knew he did not have a chance of winning the hand of dark Cathlin. He admired her from afar until his parent's nagging finally forced him to choose a wife from among the other farm folk in the area. Phillip settled onto a piece of land near his parent's farm with the comely but rather plump Minerva, and life went on much as usual. Phillip missed his dark Cathlin, but his wife was a good cook and had a mild manner, and he found himself spending more time at home with Minerva and less time in town pining for the colonel's daughter.

Then one day Minerva caught her husband staring at the fair, dark Cathlin as she walked past their wagon, and heard his soft sigh of longing. At once, a terrible, jealous rage tore through Minerva. From that moment, she began to ridicule and mock the colonel's daughter whenever Cathlin's name was mentioned, and she kept track of her husband in such a distrustful, nagging manner that Phillip's life became a sheer misery to him.

Phillip's thoughts turned more and more frequently to beautiful, dark Cathlin. He began going to town each day in the hope of seeing his beloved as she went about her daily tasks. Sometimes he spoke to her, and he treasured the memory of her words long after they parted, replaying them again and again in his mind.

When he was not lurking in the town, Phillip went out deer hunting with his two prize-winning hounds. He spent most of his time away from home, neglecting all but the most necessary of his farm tasks and avoiding contact with his wife. Whenever he did return to his house, Minerva nagged him and complained so much that he quickly found another excuse to leave.

One evening, after a good day of hunting, Phillip and his two dogs bunked down for the night in the hunting lodge he had built on the side of the mountain. He dressed and hung the stags he had killed, fed himself and his hounds, then settled down in his bunk to sleep. Suddenly, the door creaked open, and a beautiful large heath hen picked its way over to the fire and sat down beside it. Phillip's hounds stirred and looked at the bird, but they decided it was harmless and uninteresting, so they went back to sleep.

As Phillip lazily watched the creature fluffing its feathers before the fire, the bird began to swell. Phillip drew in a startled breath as the heath hen grew larger and larger. In a few minutes, it had reached the size of a human being, and its form soon settled into that of an old woman wearing a brown cloak and a peaked hat with a wide brim. It was a hex—a female witch!

The hex stalked over to Phillip's bunk and towered above him. Her movements wakened the hounds, and they leaped up and growled at this stranger threatening their master.

DARK CATHLIN

"Call off your dogs," the hex said to Phillip, "for I mean you no harm."

Her voice was strangely soft and young for such an ugly old hex. Phillip was confused but suspicious.

"I cannot make them mind," he lied to the old woman.

She plucked a strand of her wiry gray hair and handed it to him. "Tie them with this magic hair, and they will mind you," she said. Her voice was low and alluring, and for a moment, Phillip thought he glimpsed a much younger face underneath the brim of the huge hat. He glanced down at the hair in his hand. It was now long and straight and black as coal, though the hair on the crone's head was curly and gray.

Phillip pretended to tie up his dogs with the magic hair, but he really used a flimsy piece of twine from his pocket instead. He silently signaled his well-trained dogs to mind him and sit still. When she was sure the dogs were controlled, the hex reached down into the bunk and took Phillip by the shoulders. Her darkened visage drew close to him as if she were going to kiss him. Or rip his face off. Her dark eyes glimmered down at him, glowing with tiny sparks as if the stars of heaven were in their depths. Phillip was entranced . . . and terrified. He could not be sure what her intentions were, and he could not make out whether she was truly an old crone come to kill him or a young woman in disguise.

He signaled to his dogs, and immediately they snapped the flimsy piece of twine and sprang upon the stranger, snarling and ripping at her legs and body. The hex gave a shriek of pain and fear. She sprang away from the bunk, and the dogs chased her outside. Phillip heard her beating at them with a stick as they attacked her again and again. With a final shriek of agony and loss, the hex escaped from the dogs and disappeared into the night.

Shaken by his narrow escape, Phillip hurried home with his dogs as soon as it was light. He was met at the door by Minerva, who was glowing with triumph. Dark Cathlin, she informed him, was gravely ill and feared to be dying. She was on her way to minister to the sick girl, as was her Christian duty, and she insisted that her wayward husband join her, hoping that the sight of the dying dark Cathlin would wound him as deeply as he had wounded his lawfully wedded wife with his sighs for the colonel's daughter.

When they reached the colonel's home, they found the doors barred to them. But Minerva was determined and soon overrode the protests of the servants. She bore her husband into the house and up the stairs to the bedroom of the dying dark Cathlin. The beautiful black-haired girl lay upon her face, her body writhing in agony. When he saw his love in such a state, Phillip moaned and rushed to her side.

Dark Cathlin turned her head and gaze up at him with fathomless deep eyes that glimmered with tiny sparks as if the stars of heaven were in their depths. Phillip recognized her eyes immediately and groaned aloud as he realized that it was she who had come to him in the night, disguised first as a heath hen and then as a crone. He threw back the blankets that covered her and saw the terrible wounds that his dogs had inflicted upon her flesh.

Minerva, seeing the look that passed between her husband and the beautiful, dying dark Cathlin, was overcome with jealous rage. Drawing a knife from her waistband, she thrust it into the back of the lovely hex, killing her instantly. Phillip gave a shout of rage and turned upon his wife, who fled immediately. Phillip followed one step, two, then paused and turned back to gather the body of his beloved dark Cathlin in his arms for the first and last time.

Mad with grief and sorrow, Phillip left his wife for the army, where he tried to numb his pain with endless work. But he could not shake off the memory of dark Cathlin, who had silently returned his love and whose death he had caused in his ignorance. Finally, he deserted the army and went deep into the woods where the girl lay buried, taking with him the sacred books used by the powwow doctors. For many nights, Phillip tried to raise the spirit of dark Cathlin, but she would not return.

Two months following the death of his beloved, Phillip hanged himself from a large tree that grew near her grave. That night, a great storm raged over the town and forest, and the wind swirled around and around the body of Phillip. The branches of the tree were tossed back and forth as if they were beautiful strands of long black hair, and the howling wind seemed to have the echo of an alluring woman's voice within its depths. After the storm, when the townsfolk came to cut the poor farmer down from the tree, they found a smile of pure happiness upon his dead face. Phillip and his dark Cathlin were together at last.

The Walking Statue

LANCASTER CITY

Augusta could hear them arguing right through the floor of her bedroom. She huddled in the center of her huge bed, watching the firelight flicker through the deep crimson curtains of the canopy and listening bitterly. They were debating whether or not to attend her wedding the following morning. Augusta still did not understand why they disapproved of Tevis. He was hard-working, honest, and came from a decent family. She considered herself very lucky to have found him, and the early days of their courtship were among her happiest memories.

Then the time had come to introduce Tevis to her family. It was a disaster from the moment he entered their parlor. Her parents thought he was too low class for her. They criticized everything about him, from his warm, open manners to the way he spoke and the way he dressed. For the first time in her life, Augusta had defied her parents and kept seeing Tevis. The day that she became engaged to him, there had been a terrible argument, first between her and her father, then between her and her mother, and a third fight late that night between her mother and father.

139

In spite of all the objections, Augusta had insisted upon marrying Tevis. Her fiancé hated coming between her and her parents and did everything in his power to reconcile them. But they were intractable. For one long, bitter night, Augusta had debated with herself, trying to decide between her family and Tevis. Then, the next morning, Tevis had smiled at her and touched her face as he helped her tenderly down from his carriage, and in that moment, Augusta knew deep in her heart that she would do anything to be with him.

Slowly her parents' argument faded away, to be replaced by silence. Augusta sighed deeply and lay back against her pillows. Tomorrow, she would leave this house for the last time and never return. The thought made her glad. She cuddled a pillow to her chest and dozed lightly, dreaming of Tevis.

Augusta woke suddenly in the middle of the night, aware of a terrible thirst. She reached for the water glass that she kept on the table beside her bed, but it was empty. Thrusting her feet into slippers, she padded out into the hallway, not bothering to take a candle with her. She knew the way to the kitchen very well, even in the dark.

As Augusta descended the steps to the first floor, her foot slipped on the fresh coat of floor varnish that had been used to polish the stairs earlier that evening. She gasped, desperately waving her arms, trying to catch the railing. Her flailing hand missed their target, and she plunged toward the floor, bouncing painfully off the steps. On the second bounce, a horrible, final pain ripped through her, and she heard her neck snap. Then darkness descended upon her. She was dead before she reached the bottom of the stairs.

Augusta did not know how long it was from the moment she died to the moment her spirit returned to the graveyard where her body lay buried. It might have been days, weeks, years. Time worked very differently where her spirit now resided.

But suddenly she felt the call of the physical realm very strongly, and so she descended to the graveyard, curious to know exactly what it was that had summoned her. She found her tomb immediately and considered it for a moment. The monument that graced the top of her grave had a statue of a beautiful woman descending a short staircase. The words chiseled into the tombstone read COULD LOVE HAVE KEPT HER? Augusta frowned slightly, wondering if this grand treatment was her parents' way of apologizing for their disapproval of her marriage to Tevis.

The thought of Tevis sent a terrible pang through her. Suddenly, she longed to see him, to know what had happened to him. And then she knew what had summoned her back to earth. She glanced around the darkness, then finally saw the still form lying in the grass at the base of her tomb. Tevis had cried himself to sleep and lay silently with one hand clasped around the edge of her monument. The moonlight shone on his face, lighting up the beloved features. Augusta longed to touch him, to comfort him.

After a moment's thought, Augusta's spirit entered the statue on top of her grave. The statue sprang to life, and Augusta opened its eyes. Slowly, she descended the staircase and slipped off the monument. With a look of tenderness, she bent over the form of her beloved Tevis and gently touched his cheek. Tevis opened his eyes sleepily and gazed up at her.

THE WALKING STATUE

"Augusta?" he murmured, not yet completely awake. She nodded the statue's head. With a gasp, Tevis flung himself upward and grabbed the statue around the neck. Augusta put the statue's arms around her beloved, and they clung together for a long time.

Finally, Tevis drew away and stared deeply into the statue's now-living eyes. "Are you all right, my beloved?" he asked.

"I am all right," Augusta told him. "Do not be sad. We will be together again some day."

Tevis nodded and wiped the tears from his face. Taking him by the hand, Augusta strolled with him through the cemetery. Tevis told his beloved that it was exactly one year from the day she had slipped and fallen to her death. He had come to spend this anniversary at her grave, since they could not spend it together. He kept glancing shyly over at the statue, amazed and overjoyed at this miracle that allowed him to speak to her again.

After an hour spent in this manner, Augusta could feel her spirit being called back to the eternal realm. Reluctantly, she bade Tevis farewell and walked back up onto the monument. A moment later, the statue froze into place. Augusta was gone.

In the fullness of time, Tevis left this life, and his spirit was reunited with his beloved fiancée. But from that day to this, the statue of Augusta continues to descend from her monument on the anniversary of her death and stroll through the graveyard in memory of the life that was cut short on the eve of her wedding.

23

Top Hat

SCHUYLKILL HAVEN

The nurse glimpsed the man here and there as she went about her nightly duties. He was tall and slender, and he dressed in fancy, old-fashioned black clothes, culminating in a high silk hat that covered his black hair and shaded his face so that she never caught a glimpse of it.

Mostly, she saw him at night, striding through the halls as if he owned them, though occasionally he would appear during the day. Usually he was on the far side of the ward, entering a room as she was leaving. He was never close enough for her to speak to him, not that she would have ever presumed to address him; his manner was standoffish, to say the least.

Still, he intrigued her. The nurse began calling him "Top Hat" on account of the tall silk hat he always wore upon his head. "He reminds me of Abraham Lincoln," she told her fellow nurses during their break. None of her friends had ever seen the dark man, though they watched for him nightly and speculated as to his origins and his strange attire.

"Perhaps he is an undertaker, trying to drum up some new business," mused an intern friend over her coffee.

"Too tacky," an administrative aide replied, tossing her curly brown head and grinning at the nurse. "I know! He comes from a large family . . . "

"A large, sickly family," the intern inserted with a grin.

"A large sickly family," the administrative aide agreed. "And he is always coming to the hospital to visit them."

"Maybe he's a ghost!" the intern said. She gave a deep, spectral laugh and waved her hands for emphasis.

The nurse giggled along with her friends as she washed her coffee cup out in the sink. Then she went back on duty with a cheerful grin on her face. A ghost, eh? Perhaps a doctor who lost one too many patients in life and had returned to do penance after death?

It was nearly midnight when the nurse looked up from her paperwork and saw Top Hat striding down the hall. She gasped aloud and shivered, though there was nothing particularly menacing about the tall figure in black. He turned abruptly and entered one of the rooms on her ward. The nurse stood up, shaking a little. There was a deathly ill woman in that room who was not expected to last the night. Everything had already been done to make her comfortable, and the nurse checked on her every few minutes. Supposedly, the woman had no family. But here was Top Hat come to see her, even though visiting hours were over long ago. Perhaps he was a minister.

The nurse walked casually down the hall, not quite sure what to do. If Top Hat were a family member, then it was more than appropriate for him to be at the woman's side as she passed into the next life. Ditto if he were a minister. But what if he were not a relation or a clergyman? She would have to evict him from the room. The thought of approaching the dark figure in the tall silk hat made her feel ill.

The nurse walked slowly past the room, glancing inside as she did. There he was, a tall black figure standing silently at the foot of the woman's bed. His complete stillness was uncanny. His face was shadowed by the tall hat, and the nurse was glad of it. She was not sure she could bear to look directly at this terrible figure. He gazed in silence down at the woman on the bed, making no move to take her hand or comfort her final hours. He just waited.

The nurse turned at the end of the hall and approached the room again. She would have to go inside and confront the man. But when she neared the door, her flesh broke out into a cold, clammy sweat, and her legs turned to jelly. The feeling of nausea overwhelmed her. She caught a glimpse of the dark figure at the foot of the bed briefly as she raced past the room on her way to the bathroom, where she vomited into a toilet.

When she emerged from the bathroom, the nurse spent a few minutes composing herself. The she walked along the ward, checking on each patient in turn, her eyes always returning to the door of the dying woman. As she drew near, she felt a warning twinge of nausea, and so she kept walking, allowing herself only a sideways glance into the room. Top Hat stood silent and still at the foot of the bed, waiting.

The nurse slowly went back to her post, her eyes fixed on the dying woman's door. Every time she thought about approaching the room and confronting the man inside, the nausea returned, and her whole body became clammy with a cold sweat. She would have to wait until Top Hat left and then check on the patient.

TOP HAT

Suddenly, the buzzers and bells from the dying woman's room went off all at once. Fear and nausea forgotten in her call to duty, the nurse raced down the hall toward the room, determined to evict Top Hat and stabilize her patient if it was humanly possible. She ran into the room and skidded to a halt with a gasp. Top Hat was nowhere to be seen! She had not once removed her eyes from the door, and the room was windowless. There was no place to hide. So where was the tall, ominous figure in black?

The alarms were still going off. Throwing off her amazement, the nurse rushed to her patient and found that the woman was dead. Her instructions were clear: No emergency measures were to be taken to revive her, at the patient's request. Slowly, the nurse turned off the alarms and removed the equipment that had helped to keep the woman alive.

As she completed her sad task, she felt someone's eyes upon her. She looked up and out the door. Standing in the hall was a dark, skeletal figure in a tall, black silk hat. At his side was the ethereal figure of a woman, whom he held by the hand. Top Hat bowed to the nurse, and the ghost of the dead woman gave the nurse a cheerful smile and a wave. Then they were gone.

24

Angel in the Coal Mine

LANSFORD

Winter was always the worst, Max mused to himself as he bent over his bed in the darkness and kissed his sleeping wife on the forehead. He rose in the darkness of 5:00 A.M., descended at 6:00 into the damp, dripping, dust-choked darkness of the coal mine to work his eight- to ten-hour shift, then ascended into the darkness of early night.

Max quickly checked to make sure he had everything he needed for the day's mining: hand machine for drilling, drill, scraper, needle, blasting barrel, crowbar, pick, shovel, hammer, sledge, cartridge pin, oil can, toolbox, lamp, powder, squibs, paper, soap, and oil. With a small sigh, he tucked his lunch box under his arm, shouldered his toolbox, and set off for work. It was a hard life, but it was the only life he knew.

Max's next-door neighbor and best friend, Barney, was waiting on the walk outside. Calling a greeting, he fell into step with Max, and they strolled together down the road toward the mine. They were swiftly joined by the other men on their shift, and greetings, stories, and jokes were exchanged with the casual ease of old friends.

Max nodded hello to Jacob, the door boy as he walked through the entrance of the mine. Jacob had an easy but monotonous job, he mused. Jacob's duty was to open and shut the door as men and cars passed through. The doors helped control and regulate the ventilation of the mine. Poor Jacob was alone in the darkness and silence all day, save when other men and boys passed through his portal. Max tossed a piece of whittling wood he had found to the boy, who grinned cheerfully at him in thanks, showing a gap where he had lost a front tooth in a fight.

At the foot of the shaft, Max and the other workers were greeted by a red-haired young driver who stood next to a clean and rather obstinate-looking mule. Abe had just been promoted from door boy to driver, and he was very proud of his new job. The coal cars and the mule's harness sparkled in the lantern light, and Max wondered if the boy actually polished the line of coal cars to which the creature was attached.

Abe's job was to take the empty cars to the working places and return them to the foot of the shaft once the miners had loaded them with coal. The cars were then hoisted to the surface and conveyed to the breaker, where the coal was cracked, sorted, and cleaned by the breaker boy, and made ready for the market.

Max walked a mile underground until he reached his place of work. He carefully checked the propping he had put in place the day before to ensure that the roof was secure against the day's blasting, then moved deeper into the shaft to consider where to place his shots. He worked slowly and carefully. A miner who did not use his best judgment when locating and boring a hole or in preparing and determining the size of his shot was very quickly a dead miner. The number of blasts Max set off per day ranged from four to twelve, according to the size and character of the vein of coal he was working.

Max paused only once during the day to eat lunch with his laborer, Jeff. Max had hired Jeff, with his superintendent's approval, to load the cars with the coal that he blasted each day from the vein he was working. He had known the boy since he was a squalling infant in his mother's arms and had been delighted to offer him a position when his former laborer had succumbed to pneumonia earlier that year. Jeff was paid per carload; five cars full of coal—approximately 12 tons—equaled a day's work. The work was often difficult because of the dripping and standing water that was a natural part of the coal veins they worked together. But Jeff was always ready with a smile or a joke, and he made life bearable down in the dusty, damp darkness of the coal mine.

Max was exhausted by the time the last blast was cleared, and he and Jeff made their way back to the surface. They were later than usual, and the rest of the shift had already left when they emerged from the shaft and hurried out the door. With a cheerful wave, Jeff made his way to the local pub, and Max headed for home. As usual, Matilda had candles and lanterns blazing in every window to welcome him. She was the only person in the world who knew that Max was afraid of the dark.

Matilda came running to the door when he entered, throwing herself into his arms with the same enthusiasm she had shown the day he proposed marriage, and covering his dust-covered, blackened mouth with kisses. His little son and daughter followed suit, and soon the whole family was covered with coal dust. Max had often tried to dissuade Matilda from dirtying her clothes this way, but she playfully refused to listen to him.

"Clothes I can wash anytime," she told him, "but every day you come home safely to me is a day to celebrate."

Max knew she was right. As a miner, the daily dangers he faced were many. He could be crushed to death at any time by a falling roof, burned to death by exploding gas, or blown to pieces by a premature blast. Not many old men are found in the mines. The average age of those killed was thirty-two; Max had turned thirty-two on his last birthday. Though she never said a word about it, Max knew that Matilda worried about him constantly.

After washing off the dust of the mine, Max settled down to a wonderful roast beef dinner and listened happily as his four-year-old daughter and two-year-old son talked and talked about their day.

"We saw the Black Maria today," his daughter announced over dessert. Max stiffened and looked up quickly from his pie, alarmed by this news. Matilda met his glance, surprised by his ignorance of the matter. Then her eyes darkened with pain and sorrow, and Max braced himself for bad news.

The Black Maria was a covered wagon, pulled by a team of horses that was used as an ambulance or a hearse by the mine. When folks heard the mine whistle sound the alarm and then saw the Black Maria coming up the street, the wives of the miners came out onto their porches or stoops and prayed that the ambulance would pass on by.

Miners who were seriously hurt were taken by horse and carriage up to Ashland. It was a long trip over rough roads, and many miners died on the way due to the rough ride or the length of time it took to get to the hospital. If the mine officials thought that a miner would not survive the trip to the hospital, the Black Maria would bring the man to his home so that his wife could make him comfortable for the short time remaining to him. If the miner were dead, the driver would place him on the front porch of his home, and friends or neighbors would come over and prepare the deceased miner for his wake.

Max gazed questioningly at his wife, his heart sinking with fear. Who had been in the Black Maria today? Matilda bit her lip in distress and took a deep breath to calm herself. "Barnabas Johnston was killed by a blast late this afternoon," she said at last. "I thought you knew."

Max was stunned. He had been working in a remote part of the mine and had heard nothing of the accident. No wonder the supervisor had looked grim as they hurried out of the mine. For a moment, Max wondered why the super hadn't spoken to him; then he realized that his boss must have assumed, like Matilda, that he already knew.

"The wake is tomorrow night," Matilda continued gently, carefully looking away from the tears rolling silently down his cheeks. His little daughter slid down from her chair and came to curl up on his lap. His small son came and hugged his leg tightly. Max drew a deep breath to calm himself, hugged his children tightly, then asked after Barney's wife.

As she cleaned up from dinner, Matilda told him about the accident and the neighborhood reaction to the death of one of their own. There was a sad fatalism in her voice as she spoke. This had happened before and would happen again. Unspoken between them was her fear that one day the man in the Black Maria would be him. Max could picture his wife crouching terrified on their front porch, watching the ambulance make its way down their street.

Max slept poorly that night, and for many nights following his friend's death. He and Matilda did everything they could to ease their neighbor's sorrow and difficulties, loaning the widow money, watching over her children, and helping her to contact relatives who eventually offered the family a home in a distant part of the state. Gradually, life returned to normal, and a new mining family with two children close in age to their own moved in next door.

A month following Barney's death, Max was preparing to set off a new blast deep within a dark shaft of the coal mine when suddenly a brilliant light, bright as the sun, burst into being a few yards from where he stooped over the drill hole. The light shone off each speck of coal dust in the air, turning them to glitter. Mystified, Max stood upright, his eyes dazzled by the brilliance. He could make out a figure standing in the middle of all of the light. It was beckoning to him. Instinctively, Max moved toward the shining, beautiful figure with the serene countenance and the soft flutter of wings at its shoulders. From behind him, moments too soon, came the roar of an explosion. It knocked Max off his feet, and he heard a crack and a rumble as the ceiling of his excavation caved in.

Max threw his arms up to protect his head as the rock fell all around him, striking his body again and again. The light from the glowing figure surrounded him, acting as a shield that sheltered him from the worst of the cave-in. Gradually, the glow faded, the

ANGEL IN THE COAL MINE

thunder of the falling stone ceased, and Max found himself buried to the waist in rubble. His right leg throbbed painfully, and a few ribs felt sore, but none of his injuries seemed to be fatal. Jeff came running up with Abe, the driver of the coal car, shouting his name.

"I'm here," Max called to his frantic coworkers.

The two young men hurried over to him, carefully placed their lanterns down, and began the long process of digging him out. Max could see several huge pieces of coal lying only a foot away from his body, and he wondered how many of them might have struck him if it hadn't been for the beautiful figure in white. The place where he had laid the charge was completely gone, and he knew that if he had not seen the beckoning figure, he would have been killed instantly by the early blast. It was a miracle.

His right leg was broken, and he had a few bruised ribs, but otherwise Max was fine. The superintendent called him a lucky son-of-a-gun and wanted to send him home in the Black Maria. Remembering Matilda's reaction to the Black Maria, Max refused the ride. He hitched a lift home in the cart of a local farmer, escorted by Jeff. The neighbors saw him first, and soon everyone was out on their porch, calling to him and cheering when they heard he was all right. Matilda came running up the street, tears streaming down her face, clambered up into the wagon, and kissed him in front of everyone. Jeff helped him into the house, and a couple of the local workers who had rudimentary first aid training helped set his broken leg.

Max told the story of the angel who rescued him over and over again to anyone who would listen. Matilda was convinced that it was the spirit of his friend Barney returned to save him from a similar fate. Clinging tightly to his children with one arm and his wife with the other, Max just smiled and thanked God for sparing his life.

25

Corpse Candle

POTTSVILLE

It was summer, and the boys often played baseball in the empty section of the graveyard that had not yet been used. They had divided themselves up into teams called the Specters and the Ghouls, in laughing reference to their oddly placed baseball field. The competition between the two sandlot teams was fierce. The Ghouls had won the last two games in their impromptu baseball season, and the Specters were eager to win back their lead. A big game was arranged for the following Saturday.

The afternoon of the game arrived, and the two teams assembled and began battling it out for first place. The Specters took an early lead, but the Ghouls tied it up in the bottom of the seventh inning, and it was still tied in the ninth. Dusk was falling, but the boys ignored it, determined to play to the bitter end.

The extra inning was tense. The Ghouls were the home team that day, and so they had the edge. Then scrawny Eric Madison of the Specters hit a three-run homer, putting his team in the lead. The Ghouls were nervous when they came up to bat, and sure enough, it was one-two-three and they were out. The

Specters shouted and jumped around madly in their glee.

Suddenly, Eric stopped jumping and pointed through the gathering darkness toward the oldest section of the graveyard. "What's that?" he called. The other boys stopped their antics and turned to look. A blue light had appeared in the middle of the old gravestones. It was hovering several feet above the ground, but the boys could see no one holding it. From the place they were standing, the light appeared like the flame of a candle.

The boys stood motionless, gazing at the blue light. They all felt a strange, nameless dread at the mysterious sight. One by one, they shivered and clutched their arms or put their hands into their pockets to warm them.

"What is it?" Eric asked again, as the light slowly drifted deeper into the graveyard.

The other boys shook their heads, wordless. Then the newest team member, a curly-haired, dark-eyed boy whose family had just moved to the United States from Wales, said slowly: "It is a canwll corfe. A corpse candle."

Eric swallowed nervously. "What's a corpse candle?"

"Corpse candles are phosphorescent lights seen floating through the air at night. They are believed to be harbingers of death. Mam said they come to warn of the death of those who see them, or of someone close to them," said the Welsh lad. "Blue lights are usually the candles of children doomed to die, and white lights are for adults. Mam saw a white corpse candle hovering above her parents' house the night before my grand-pappy died."

"That's silly," one of the other boys said quickly, and laughed a little. No one joined him.

CORPSE CANDLE

"Sometimes," said the Welsh boy softly, "if you watch closely, you can see the funeral procession."

The boys moved closer together, their eyes fixed on the blue glow. As the light grew brighter in the gathering darkness, they began to hear the murmur of voices, the drone of a minister's voice giving a eulogy, and soft, heart-rending weeping. For a moment, the boys saw shadowy figures following the blue light as it wound its way deep into the graveyard and hovered over an empty place among the tombstones. The ghostly figures of the mourners were misty and indistinct, though there was no mistaking the air of sorrow and grief that surrounded them. The boys could make out a mother figure being supported by a tall man, and several children clustered behind them.

The sight of the ghostly funeral procession was too much for the Specters and the Ghouls. With cries of terror, the boys ran from the graveyard, scattering for home once they were safely out of the graveyard.

Three days later, the Welsh boy's infant sister died in her sleep. When they heard the news, the members of the Ghouls and the Specters were saddened, but not surprised. One by one, they stopped by their friend's house to offer him support and sympathy, their words awkward but sincere.

A week to the day after the boys had seen the corpse candle, the Welsh family buried their infant daughter in the spot where the blue corpse candle had appeared.

26

The Storm Hag

ERIE

"She lurks below the surface of the lake near Presque Isle," his uncle once told him, "her lithe form forever swimming through the weeds and the mire. Pale and green of skin, her yellow eyes shine luminously in the dark, and her thin, long arms wrap themselves around the unwary, while foul-green pointed teeth sink into soft flesh, and sharp nails at the end of long, bony fingers stroke you into the deepest sleep there is."

"What is she?" he had asked, his eyes wide with amazement and fear.

"She is known by many names," his uncle said, "but to sailors of Lake Erie, she is the Storm Hag."

He was only a young boy when his uncle first told him about the Storm Hag. Over the years, his uncle told him more. The creature was a sea witch, his uncle said, an evil Jenny Greenteeth who summoned the storms and pulled shipwrecked sailors down into her evil embrace to live with her forever at the bottom of the lake. Sometimes she would wait until the calm right after the storm to attack. When the sailors relax their guard, lulled into thinking that the danger had passed with the storm, the Storm

Hag would burst forth from the dark waters of the lake, spewing forth lightning and wind like venom. And the ship would vanish—never to be seen again.

As he grew older, he realized that the Storm Hag was just a fairy tale told to amuse and frighten a little boy. His uncle came from Scotland and told many stories of bogie men and witches. With the scorn of young adulthood, he discarded all of his uncle's tales and warnings, taking his 24-foot sailboat out into rough seas. He gloried in the unexpected gales that sprang up on Lake Erie and loved to test his seamanship against the storms.

One evening, after a difficult day at work, he decided to take a sail on the lake. There was a small craft warning out, but he was an expert sailor and took no heed. Soon he was in the deep waters, buffeted this way and that by the wind and the waves and enjoying every moment. The sky was darkening into night when he saw the ominous storm clouds gathering together on the horizon. The wind grew damp and chill, and he felt the first twinge of fear. He had sailed far out on the lake, and the storm was coming quickly. Turning his boat, he took down the sail, started the engine, and hurried toward Presque Isle and safety.

The storm caught him halfway home, and it took all his wits and strength to stay afloat. Rain lashed his body, soaking him to the skin and getting into his eyes until he couldn't see. Around him, the wind shrieked and gurgled and howled. Amid the chaos, he though he heard the sound of a voice crooning:

Come into the water, love,
Dance beneath the waves,
Where dwell the bones of sailor lads
Inside my saffron cave.

It was a trick of the storm, he told himself, tightening his grip on the wheel. Then he saw a grotesque but lithesome form rise from the waves off the port bow. A catlike green face with a squashed nose, glowing yellow eyes, and long teeth was framed by seaweed-strewn hair that writhed like sea eels. Sharp spikes protruded from the spine, and the body was covered with green scales. In place of legs, the figure had a long fish tail. It was the Storm Hag. Her arms stretched longingly toward him through the raging storm, and she beckoned to him with bony fingers.

"Come into the water, love," she crooned. "Dance beneath the waves."

"Get out of here," he shouted desperately. "Leave me alone!"

She swam closer, and he turned the wheel as hard as he could in alarm. A giant wave broadsided him, nearly tipping the boat. He fought fiercely with the recalcitrant wheel and finally regained control. The Storm Hag laughed at his dilemma and started singing again: "Come into the water, love, / Dance beneath the waves."

She was keeping pace with the boat, and he knew that the evil creature was toying with him. Heart pounding with fear, he grabbed a bait bucket and hurled it through the howling wind and rain toward the Storm Hag. The bucket hit the creature in the head, knocking her backward for a moment. She gave a shriek of anger and pain, clapping a clawed hand to her injured head. Then she disappeared beneath the pounding waves.

With a shout of triumph, he gunned the motor and turned the boat for Presque Isle and safety. He was almost within hailing distance of the island when the storm ceased as abruptly as it had

THE STORM HAG

started. The rain and wind died away to nothing, and the waves began to calm down to a more manageable level. He glanced around fearfully, but there was no sign of the Storm Hag, and he knew that he had won through to safety. Thank God for bait buckets, he thought fervently.

At that moment, the boat gave a strange lurch and began moving backward. The wheel twitched under his hands and then spun around and around, out of control. He tried to grab it, but it was moving so fast it nearly broke his arms, and he let go. He glanced around fearfully, and realized that his boat was caught up in a massive whirlpool that had sprung up just off the island. Around and around his boat swirled, floating backward into an ever smaller circle while a strange wind blew around him, small waves splashed over the bow, and droplets of mist clouded his eyes.

From the bottom of the whirlpool, a sweet voice began to croon:

Come into the water, love,
Dance beneath the waves,
Where dwell the bones of sailor lads
Inside my saffron cave.

He gave a shriek of terror as he realized that he was once again in the clutches of the Storm Hag. And then he saw her, rising out of the swirling whirlpool, her arms outstretched toward him.

"Come into the water, love," she shouted, wrapping her arms around him. He uttered one cry of sheer horror as her foul-green pointed teeth sank into the soft flesh of his face, and her sharp nails stroked down his back, tearing the skin away from his bones.

Moments later, the whirlpool was gone, and there was only the harsh beating of storm waves against the island that lessened as the wind died away to nothing. The boat and its young owner vanished without a trace, and only his uncle ever suspected the truth behind the disappearance.

27

The Jersey Devil Returns

I didn't get a chance to look at the paper until after dinner, when my wife went over to the Hilks' place to borrow something she needed for tomorrow's baking. Sitting down in my favorite chair in the kitchen, I put on my glasses and picked up the paper. Then I dropped it in disgust. The Jersey Devil was all over the headlines, again! Honestly, you would have thought people would have grown tired of the whole thing by now. But no; it had been spotted again yesterday. Apparently, the critter had flown all over southern New Jersey during the afternoon and evening hours. There were sightings in West Collingswood, Westville, and Camden, to name a few towns.

The editors of the paper had thoughtfully included a sketch of the Jersey Devil. According to the picture, it was a tall, horned creature with a thick neck, short front legs, longer legs at the rear, hooved feet, glowing eyes, a strong pair of wings, and a forked tail. Picking up the paper again, I settled back in my chair and read all about it. Folks were really frightened by the Jersey Devil and were trying to hunt it down, with no success. Personally, I felt sorry for the creature. It finally decided to show itself to the public again—its first appearance in a decade—and everyone was trying to kill it or chase it away.

At first I was surprised that the Jersey Devil had crossed the Delaware River and was cavorting about in Pennsylvania. I'd jokingly told my wife they were going to have to change its name if it kept coming over here. But the majority of the sightings remained in New Jersey, and the Jersey Pinelands were supposedly its natural habitat, so the Jersey Devil it remained.

The "history" of the Jersey Devil was as follows. In 1735, Mother Leeds was brought to bed in childbirth during a raging storm. The room was full of womenfolk gathered to help her, more out of curiosity than goodwill. They had all heard the rumors that Mother Leeds was involved in witchcraft and had sworn that instead of giving birth to a thirteenth child, she would give birth to a devil.

Tension mounted when at last the baby arrived. To the relief of most—and the disappointment of some—the baby was completely normal. But a few moments later, before the women's terrified eyes, the child began to change. The room filled with screams as the child grew at an enormous rate, becoming taller than a man and changing into a beast that resembled a dragon, with beady eyes and a long snout, a snake-like body, and bat wings.

As soon as it was full-grown, the monster began beating the women (including his mother) with its thick, forked tail. With a harsh cry, it flew through the chimney and vanished into the storm. After that, the Jersey Devil regularly haunted the Pinelands, committing all sorts of misdemeanors, such as killing farmers' livestock, poisoning pools and creeks, and disturbing the peace. Finally, some preacher took a bell, book, and candle and exorcised the Devil, sending it away for good.

At least, that was what everyone had thought, until a patrolman over in Bristol, Pennsylvania, saw the Jersey Devil while he was making the rounds of Buckley Street Saturday evening, January 16, 1909. The officer shot at the monster, but the Devil just screamed at him and flew away. It was spotted several more times that night, and during the days that followed there were reports of footprints, Devil sightings, Devil hunts, and mass hysteria.

The kitchen door burst open at this juncture in my musings. Looking over the top of the page, I saw my breathless wife leaning against the door and gasping.

"George! George! It was here!" she said. My heart sank. Oh no, not another sighting.

"What was here?" I asked, lowering the paper slightly.

"The Jersey Devil!" Carol exclaimed, waving her hands in the air for emphasis. "It landed on the loaded wagon being driven by the Hilks' farmhand, so he quickly drove into the barn and locked it inside."

"The Jersey Devil is locked in a barn down the road?" I asked incredulously, putting the newspaper down on the table. This I had to see.

"No, no. Unfortunately, it escaped," Carol said, dropping into a chair and fanning herself. "No one knows how. It's flown far away by now."

"How long ago was this?" I asked.

"About an hour ago," Carol said. "Hilk and a couple of men rowed across the river from Trenton and searched the barn for the Devil. They finished just a few minutes ago, but they could not find any sign that it had been there."

I shook my head at that but refrained from comment. It was a fantastic story, and I wasn't sure that I believed it.

"Well, I'd best check up on the cows, make sure they are settled in for the night," I said to Carol, rising from my chair and walking to the door to get my coat and cap. I always went to check on the cows when I wanted time to myself. This crazy story was something I needed time to digest.

Carol's eyes widened. "Be careful out there, Father," she said. "That Devil is still loose."

"I will," I said soothingly, refraining from making a sarcastic remark. Forty years of marriage had taught me when it was wise to hold my tongue.

I lit the lantern and started out in the snowy darkness toward the barn. As I strolled along, I spotted some strange tracks in the untrodden snow in the pasture. They looked like the tracks of a huge two-footed cat, except one foot was slightly larger than the other. I stopped abruptly and studied them. I'd never seen anything like them before.

The hair on my arms pricked, and I shivered suddenly, remembering Carol's story about the Jersey Devil who had just been seen on the next farm. I resumed walking, glancing slowly from side to side in as casual a manner as I possibly could. A few yards from the massive old sycamore tree, the tracks ended abruptly, as if the creature had flown away. Flown away where? I wondered. Then I looked up. Seated on the thickest branch of the old tree was a tall, horned creature with a thick neck, short front legs, longer legs at the rear, glowing eyes, wings like a bat,

THE JERSEY DEVIL RETURNS

and a thick, forked tail. I stared at it, stupefied into stillness. It was the Jersey Devil.

My first thought was that the cartoonist had gotten it wrong. The creature had claws, not hooves on its feet. My second thought was, Good God, the critter is frightened! And it was. It was breathing heavily, blinking its large yellow eyes over and over again. One clawed hand was clutched tightly around a small branch, and its wings were hunched as if in pain.

My own fear melted away into pity for the large, lonely creature sitting in my tree. Imagine being yelled at, hunted, and fired upon every place you flew. No peace. No rest. It hissed softly at me but made no attempt to flee. It was obviously tired and upset.

"Well, hello there, big fellow," I said quietly, in the soothing voice I used with my horses and cows when they were ill. "Did you have a bad scare?"

The Jersey Devil twitched its ears and considered me thoughtfully for a moment. It opened its mouth and made a soft mewing sound that reminded me of a crying baby.

"You're welcome to stay in my tree as long as you like," I told the creature. "I'm going to check up on the cows and make sure everything is all right in the barn."

I turned slowly away and walked softly down the snow-packed path to the barn. I glanced back as I opened the door and saw the Jersey Devil relax on its perch, its hunched wings slowly settling onto its back and its grip on the branch loosening perceptibly. I nodded to myself and went inside.

To my surprise, none of the horses or cows seemed bothered by the large creature outside their barn. They knew it was there; they kept turning their heads toward the far side of the barn and sniffing the air inquisitively. But the Jersey Devil obviously didn't frighten them. I spoke softly to each animal in turn, gave each of them some extra hay, and paused to give Blue, my favorite horse, a final rub on the ear. Then I took up my lantern again and went outside.

I glanced immediately up into the sycamore tree and saw the motionless Devil sitting there. It had calmed considerably while I was in the barn and now perched like a contented bird, its yellow eyes almost closed and its tail wrapped loosely around the massive branch to maintain its balance.

"You know, my friend," I said in the same soothing voice I had used before, "it might be safest for you if you return to the Pine Barrens. Personally, I don't mind having you here in Pennsylvania, but there are others who would not agree with me."

The Jersey Devil opened its yellow eyes and mewed at me again. "Just a friendly suggestion," I added mildly. The Jersey Devil blinked a few times, considering me with a cocked head and an air of thoughtfulness. Then it swooped down right over my head and landed in the field behind me. I whirled to face it. The Jersey Devil bowed its head toward me, then raised its wings and hissed hopefully, showing its teeth and doing a strange little dance. Good lord, I thought, it's trying to court me!

"Sorry, fellow, but I'm already taken," I told the creature. The Jersey Devil rocked back and forth a few times, considering my words. Then it crouched low to the ground, tensed its wings for flight, and sprang into the air. It lifted gracefully up and over the trees, wings beating rhythmically. Then it was gone.

"Bye," I called, waving my free hand. Then I turned toward the house, wondering if I should tell Carol about my Jersey Devil encounter. Remembering the glee with which she had followed the Devil hunt, I decided against it. She just wouldn't understand.

Wild-fire

BANGOR

By the time she was two weeks old, it was obvious that Ginny's baby sister was very ill. It started with a painful red rash on the baby's hands and feet, but soon the redness spread to her face and then all over her body. Then the infant developed a terribly high fever that scared her family. The poor child shook with chills, vomited, and cried constantly in pain. Ginny was frightened. She already loved the little girl and didn't want her to die.

Their neighbors soon identified the disease as wild-fire. They recommended that Ginny's parents take the baby to the local powwow doctor, since there was no physician nearby, and the family could not afford to travel to the city to visit one. Ginny was frightened when she heard the news. The powwow doctor's name was Richard Johnson, and he owned the local sawmill and the blacksmith shop. All the young children were frightened of him and avoided him when they could. He was a tall man with a shock of white hair and a long white mustache. His blue eyes were hidden behind thick, round glasses, and his mouth was thin and stern.

Old Man Johnson lived in the house next to the school, and he often shouted at the schoolchildren when they picked up the apples that fell from his tree into the schoolyard. The older boys sassed him behind his back, calling him "Old Dickie" and throwing apples at his house and barn. On dark nights, the boys would run down to the sawmill and knock over the cart Old Man Johnson kept on the abandoned railroad track for hauling lumber. But no one dared mock him to his face. They had all heard the stories about the powwow man; they knew that Richard Johnson could hex folks who annoyed him.

The baby's symptoms grew worse and worse. After carefully counting her pennies, Ginny's mother gathered up Ginny, her brother, and the baby and hurried down the dirt road toward the powwow doctor's house. A neighbor's child tagged along. As they walked, Ginny twisted her hands nervously, remembering some of the stories she had heard about Old Man Johnson.

When her neighbor, young Thomas, had decided to become a hunter instead of taking a job at the local mercantile, his parents had paid Old Man Johnson to lay a hex on Thomas's gun. From the moment the hex was laid, Thomas never shot another creature. No matter how carefully he aimed, his bullets always went astray. One day, he came face to face with a huge buck. It was in point-blank range, and Thomas aimed his gun directly at its head and pulled the trigger. The gun did not fire. After that, Thomas threw the gun away and went to work in the mercantile.

Then there was the time that some of the schoolboys had snuck down to the blacksmith during recess and had watched Old Man Johnson chanting and waving over an old man's broken leg. The old man was groaning, "It hurts like anything! It hurts like anything!" which made the boys giggle and poke one another. Their laughter caught the powwow doctor's attention, and he chased them away from the smithy. Later, through the window of the schoolhouse, the boys saw the old man walking away from the blacksmith shop, completely healed.

All too soon, Ginny caught sight of the one-room school-house and the fancy, two-story house with the enclosed porch that loomed next to it. She saw the infamous apple tree; its branches, already full of tiny apples, were hanging over the fence into the schoolyard. Come autumn, those apples would fall to the ground and get the boys into trouble with Old Man Johnson.

Ginny was trembling with fear as they walked up to the front door and knocked. Her mother was in the lead with the crying baby in her arms, and Ginny was right behind her. She hugged herself tightly, wondering what Old Man Johnson was going to do to the baby. The door was opened by the elderly housekeeper, who ushered them into the darkened front parlor and went to get the powwow doctor.

Richard Johnson appeared even fiercer up close. Ginny and her brother cowered behind the couch, where her mother sat holding the baby. Old Man Johnson snapped out a few questions as he looked at the infant. Then he confirmed a diagnosis of wild-fire and instructed her mother to hold the infant up and away from her body so that he could work his healing spell upon the child.

Richard Johnson waved his hands a few inches above the infant's body, chanting words that were just mumbo-jumbo to Ginny. Then he intoned a strange rhyme in English. It sounded like a skipping rhyme, but the powwow doctor's grim expression

WILD-FIRE

and the menacing tone in his deep voice made it the scariest thing Ginny had ever heard.

Wild-fire and the dragon,
Flew over a wagon,
The wild-fire abated
And the dragon skated.

Old Man Johnson chanted the words over and over, then he went to the fireplace and pushed a shovel into the coals under the wood. Straightening, he shook several coals onto the edge of the hearth. He drew on some thick leather gloves, picked the coals up, and carried them over to the couch where her mother cowered, holding up the baby with shaking hands. Ginny gasped in horror. Was he going to burn the baby? She started to come around the side of the couch, determined to thrust herself between the mad doctor and her baby sister, but her mother shook her head, and Ginny stayed where she was.

She watched as Old Man Johnson passed his hands back and forth just above the infant's body once again, his gloves smoking from the heat of the coals. He spoke more strange words and chanted the rhyme again.

Then it was over. Money exchanged hands, and her mother carried the wailing infant along the dirt road toward home. Ginny followed with her brother, so relieved to be away from the strange house and its terrifying occupant, that she barely noticed anything else. Suddenly, her brother exclaimed excitedly, pointing at the baby. The redness was fading from her swollen face, and the bumps from the rash were starting to go down.

Ginny's mother stopped for a moment, and they all gathered around the little girl. Drops of sweat were beading the baby's forehead. Her mother felt the child's face. "Her fever has broken," she exclaimed in joyful awe. "It's broken!" She hugged the still-squalling child to her chest, her face transformed by joy. "Thank God!"

By the time they reached home, the baby's cries of pain had changed to the more urgent demands for food. Ginny's mother fed her, washed her, and then laid her down to the first peaceful sleep she had enjoyed since the rash appeared on her body. Within two days, the baby was completely cured.

There were two memories that remained vivid in Ginny's mind about the incident, long after the powwow doctor was dead and gone and she was a mother herself. The first was the fear she had felt as she entered Old Man Johnson's porch and wondered what he would do to the baby; the second was the look on her mother's face when they realized that the baby had been healed.

The Dragon Tree

LENHARTSVILLE

Well, I remember when that old, twisted, gnarled tree by the Blue Rocks in the field over yonder was as straight and tall as you please. Used to be a favorite meeting place for the neighborhood men to chew the fat or complain about their work and their wives. All the local hunts started out right underneath its branches and often ended there, too.

'Course, the women-folk nagged the fellows to find another meeting place. The gals said that anybody foolish enough to gather near the Blue Rocks was sure to find trouble. We just laughed at their silly notions. The Blue Rocks were just rocks, no matter what the local legends said.

And the local legends had quite a story to tell. Seems someone told the Devil about a vegetable called a potato that was the tastiest treat in the whole dad-blame county. Well, ol' Lucifer was unfamiliar with the vegetable in question and asked for a description. Potatoes were round and hard, he was told; some were big, and some were small.

Satisfied with this description, the Devil hied himself down to Lehigh County and started filling up his sacks with every-

182

thing round and hard he could find. He collected thousands of these hard, round objects, and was planning on collecting a thousand more. Then the bravest of his minions informed ol' Lucifer that the objects inside his sack weren't potatoes. They were rocks.

Well, that made Satan just plain mad. He had a temper tantrum that shook everything up in the whole county. He shouted and he stamped his feet and he jumped up and down. Then he ripped open those sacks and threw the rocks all over the place. The rocks landed in gullies and in rivers and on the mountains and in the fields.

A whole passel of rocks landed in the empty field near the old meeting tree. They settled deep into the ground, and no one could budge them. Since the field was no good for farming after the Devil threw his "potatoes" into it, the menfolk started using it as a local meeting place. And that's how the Blue Rocks came to rest in Lenhartsville—at least, that's how the story goes.

Now, as I was saying, the womenfolk in town were mighty superstitious and thought that anyone foolish enough to hang around in a field full of rocks put there by the Devil himself was bound to have something bad happen to him. Unfortunately for us, we found out they were right.

A bunch of us were standing around under the meeting tree one evening, discussing a recalcitrant cow one of the neighbors was trying to sell, when we heard a terrible shrieking noise coming from somewhere above us. We cast our eyes up and up over the top of the mountains and saw a fiercesome creature burst out from behind the mountain, fire trailing in its wake. It had a huge, bloated body, an angled head, a pointed snout, sharp teeth, a long, whipping tail, and broad wings. We gasped aloud when we saw it. It was a dragon!

It was then that I remembered the other old legend from around these parts that spoke of the Devil's pet that lived in a *drachelechar*—a dragon's cave—beneath the mountains, only coming out when hunger wakened it from its deep sleep. It had not always been a dragon, the legend claimed. Once it was a Native American warrior who loved a maiden fair. Forbidden by her father to wed the man she desired, the maiden leaped from a cliff and died upon the rocks at its base. Stricken with grief, the warrior retreated to a cave deep in the mountain, and there he was transformed by the Devil into a fiery dragon who would soar out above the mountains and wreak vengeance upon his enemies. The girl's father, who had forbidden the match, was the first to die.

I trembled when I saw the dragon dancing so gracefully upon the night air, wondering if the Devil's pet would try to claim the Devil's Potato Patch where we stood as part of its territory. We might not be the only ones who started our hunts from this spot!

As I watched in awe and terror, the dragon pumped its wings harder, flying up to the top of the mountain, where it lingered for a moment, seeming to dance upon the wind, lit by the fire that poured forth from its wicked mouth. Then it slipped down into the valley on the far side. Slowly, the sound of its shrieks died away.

We breathed a sigh of relief when the dragon disappeared. Several fellows came out from behind the tree, where they had fled at the sight of the fiery creature. We chided them for their cowardice, and they laughed with us, although their grins were rather forced.

Around us, the night grew calm and still, although the crickets and the night critters stayed silent and watchful. This should have warned us, but it didn't. We were completely unprepared for the sudden roar that came from the ridge directly above us. We whipped around and stared in disbelief as the dragon launched itself from the top of the mountain where it had crept unnoticed as we talked together. Straight toward the meeting tree it flew, and it opened its mouth to emit a stream of fearsome heat and flame.

Let me tell you, the feel of that heat woke us up. With screams of terror, all the men scattered, running for the safety of the rocks and the forest beyond. By the time the dragon reached the meeting tree, there was no sign of the prey it had been hunting. The dragon gave a piercing howl of frustration and landed in the branches of the meeting tree.

The tree gave an ear-numbing boom and cracked in two, its branches curling and withering away from the heat of the dragon perched upon it. The dragon wrapped its tail around the base of the tree and stretched its long neck up and over the once-straight branches near the top. From this position, it watched the Blue Rocks intently for any sign of movement. None came. All of us townsmen were lying flat on the ground inside the Devil's Potato Patch, not daring to breathe lest those glowing eyes spot us among the boulders.

We would have stayed that way all night if the dragon hadn't suddenly seen a small herd of deer crossing at the far end of the field. With a challenging roar, it took off from the tree and sailed over the Blue Rocks in search of an easy meal. As soon as it passed our hiding spot, we broke and ran for home.

THE DRAGON TREE

Our story was greeted with many "I told you so" remarks from our wives. We put up with it meekly, just grateful that our lives had been spared. For two more nights, the roars and shrieks of the dragon filled the mountains and valleys around our town. Then the creature returned to its *drachelechar* to sleep.

From that day on, the gnarled, cracked, ruined mess that was all that remained of the meeting tree was shunned by the local men. We began gathering on the front steps of the local mercantile, which made our womenfolk happy. After all, why risk our lives meeting at the Blue Rocks? Someday, the dragon might waken again.

30

Nevermore

FAIRMOUNT PARK,
PHILADELPHIA

All my life I have seen the Shadows. From my very earliest rec-
ollections, I have watched them as the lurked at the corners of
my vision, chuckling to themselves, and calling softly to me:
"Edgar! Edgar Allan Poe!" They were evil, I knew instinctively,
and I endeavored always to keep them at bay.

My father left us quite early, and my mother died of tuberculosis when I was two, so by the time I could speak well enough
to tell an adult about the Shadows, I was living with John Allan,
a successful tobacco merchant in Richmond, Virginia. He was a
practical man, and the family had no time for a child who shied
at Shadows, real or imaginary. So when I heard the Shadows rapping at my bedroom walls at night, I quickly learned to ignore it.
"'Tis some visitor," I would mutter, pulling the covers over my
head, "tapping at my chamber door. Only this and nothing
more."

At first, I did not see the Shadows during the day. They came
mostly during the evening when the light was dim and people
talked in lower voices. Sometimes, the Shadows would beckon to

me, trying to lure me into their darkness. I always turned away from them and hurried toward the nearest light, filled with fantastic terrors never felt before.

I was sent to boarding school in England, and the Shadows followed me there. I was a restless boy, and I already loved words. My ambition was to be a writer someday, and I used words to block out the Shadows, which appeared in unexpected places: the doorway to a classroom, behind the head of a teacher, on the ceiling at night. They stretched out unbelievably thin hands toward me and gurgled with an evil laughter that wrapped itself deep into my soul. I would roll over in my bed and stick my head under my pillow, muttering, "It is just darkness there, nothing more." The other boys thought I was strange, but they tolerated me, and that was all I asked.

I attended university for a year but had to drop out, due to gambling debts I accrued while attempting to earn some spending money. My foster father did not approve, and we had words, much to the delight of the Shadows that danced within the silken, sad, uncertain rustling of each purple curtain. I blocked out their whispers as best I could and joined the army as a private, using the name Edgar A. Perry. That same year, I released my first book, which I called *Tamerlane and Other Poems*. I was happiest when I was writing. It seemed to push the Shadows deeper into the darkness where they belonged, nameless there for evermore. For the first time, I was able to fully enjoy the light and laughter of the people around me. After serving for two years and attaining the rank of sergeant major, I was discharged from the army.

Darkness fell again upon me that year. It should have been a glorious time, for I published my second book called *Al Aaraaf*. But it was also the year that my foster mother, Frances Allan, died. Deep into death's darkness I peered, doubting and dreaming dreams no mortals ever dared to dream before. But death's silence remained unbroken, and all my vigil brought to me was cruel laughter from the Shadows. At last, I turned back from the darkness and walked toward the light, to fulfill my foster mother's death wish and reconcile with my foster father.

John Allan coordinated an appointment for me to the United States Military Academy at West Point, but this was an ill-fated step for me. I was headstrong and spirited and disinclined to obey orders, which got me dismissed from the academy. After that, the break with my foster father became permanent. All my soul within me burned at the injustice. At that moment, I was sure that I was doomed to stand alone in this world and to face the Shadows as best I could.

But Fate held something else in store for me. I received an invitation to live in Maryland with my widowed aunt, Maria Clemm, and her daughter, Virginia. I accepted it gladly. I began writing in earnest then, publishing enough fiction to support myself. Once again, the writing helped to push the Shadows away, until they were just an oily smear at the back of my eyesight, easily ignored. I began editing the *Southern Literary Messenger* for Thomas W. White in Richmond, and I married my thirteen-year-old cousin, Virginia.

When I left my job with the *Messenger,* I took my beautiful young wife with me to New York, where we sought in vain for fame and fortune. It was here that I began seeing Shadows in earnest. Their voices haunted my waking hours, and their dark faces filled my dreams. It was only with the help of my dear wife and the bottle that I kept the Shadows at bay.

After fifteen fruitless months, we left New York and moved to Philadelphia. My luck changed then. My novella, *The Narrative of A. Gordon Pym,* was published and widely reviewed. Then I became assistant editor of *Burton's Gentleman's Magazine* and went on to publish numerous articles, stories, and reviews, which helped cement my reputation as a trenchant critic that I had established when I was at the *Southern Literary Messenger.*

In one way, the Shadows proved a boon to me. I found that I could use their grim, ungainly, ghastly, gaunt, and ominous figures as inspiration for my poems and stories. Soon, I had developed a collection that was published in two volumes under the title *Tales of the Grotesque and Arabesque.* I had high hopes for financial success from this book, but it earned me little money. Finally, I left *Burton's* after about a year and found a position as assistant editor at *Graham's Magazine.*

Then my lovely wife, my Virginia, developed tuberculosis. How the Shadows did hiss and laugh and taunt me when her case was diagnosed! I lashed out at them in private, shouting, "Get thee back into the tempest and the Night's Plutonian shore!" But the Shadows grew thicker still and seemed to whisper to me: "Nevermore."

Soon, Virginia was an invalid, and I began to fear for her life. I saw the Shadows everywhere, their dark faces becoming clearer each day, their fiery eyes burning into my bosom's core. I began drinking more heavily to mute the shrieking Shadows and to soften the stress of Virginia's illness. I left *Graham's* and returned to New York, where I worked briefly at the *Evening Mirror* before becoming editor of *The Broadway Journal*. On January 29, 1845, my poem "The Raven" appeared in the *Mirror* and became a popular sensation. I was not surprised. The poem had practically been dictated by the Shadows.

In 1846, the *Broadway Journal* failed, and my ailing wife and I moved to a cottage in the Bronx. In 1847, my beloved Virginia died. It was only then that the true depth of the words I had penned in "The Raven" echoed within my soul.

> *Ah, distinctly I remember it was in the bleak December,*
> *And each separate dying ember wrought its ghost upon the floor.*
> *Eagerly I wished the morrow; —vainly I had sought to borrow*
> *From my books surcease of sorrow—sorrow for the lost Lenore—*
> *For the rare and radiant maiden whom the angels name*
>   *Lenore—*
> *Nameless here for evermore.*

After Virginia's death, the Shadows claimed me. In my lucid moments, I tried to fight my way back to light by seeking a replacement for the woman who had kept me sane. First I courted the poet Sarah Helen Whitman, but her mother was strongly against our engagement and used my drinking and erratic behavior to break us apart. I tried to commit suicide then by overdosing on laudanum, but my attempt failed. So I returned to Richmond and wooed a childhood sweetheart, seeking to find salvation through her gentle words and nature. But even her sweet face could not stave off the Shadows. Ah, the Shadows!

NEVERMORE

I returned to Philadelphia in July of 1849 and was arrested shortly after my arrival for drunkenness, though at the time I was sober. I didn't try to fight the charges. The Shadows were thick upon the walls of the station, and they hissed to me of a plot to take my life. At least in the hands of the police, I was safe.

I later found refuge with my friend Sartain, who knew me when I was the editor of *Graham's Magazine*. I told him about the plot on my life, while the Shadows sang sweetly behind his head, and I begged him for a razor to trim my mustache, thus disguising me from the assassins. Having none to offer me, he trimmed it instead with scissors.

One night after tea, the Shadows began to call to me, whispering of a moonlit walk along the Schuylkill River. A walk sounded wonderful, so I rose and stepped out into the darkness. Sartain hurried to join me, and the Shadows hissed with anger when I accepted his company. They retreated a little, back into the darkness. In their absence, I felt free to tell my friend of the words and visions they had imprinted in my mind. As we climbed the wooden steps to the lofty top of the reservoir, I described the hallucination I'd had in the prison cell, in which my mother-in-law had been dismembered before my eyes.

After my safe return from the reservoir, the Shadows came back in force. I was plagued with cholera and spasms until I could hardly hold a pen. Night after night I would pace the floor and strike out with words against the demons. "Prophet!" I shrieked at the red-eyed Shadow in the closet. "Thing of evil! Tell me truly, I implore! Is there balm in Gilead? Tell me, tell me, I implore!" And the Shadow answered, "Nevermore."

All desire to live had left me, but I kept up my restless

travels, trying to throw off the Shadows that dogged my every step. I left Philadelphia at the end of July and went down to Richmond. In October, I journeyed north once again, passing through Baltimore on my way to New York.

It was in Baltimore that I came face to face with one last Shadow. Tall as a tree, dark as ebony, facing me down on the streets of Baltimore, stood the Raven from my poem. I recognized him at once and knew that he had come for me. I threw my hands in front of my face and screamed at him the famous words that I myself had penned.

Leave no black plume as a token of that lie thy soul hath spoken!
Leave my loneliness unbroken!—quit the bust above my door!
Take thy beak from out my heart, and take thy form from off
  my door!

As the darkness claimed me, I heard the foul Raven croaking: "Nevermore."

I woke to the hustle and bustle of a hospital room. I tried to speak to the nurses, but the Shadows kept interrupting me, until all I could do was fall back on my pillows and exclaim: "Lord, help my poor soul." Then the Shadows swooped down upon me, smothering the air out of me, until I breathed my last.

A very long time later, I found my spirit walking along the Schuylkill River toward the Fairmount Water Works, the very same path I had once trodden in life with my good friend Sartain. I looked down upon myself and saw that my spirit form was made out of swirling darkness and gray mist. I groaned aloud, and my voice sounded with a ghastly hiss that ended in a terrible shriek.

I recognized the sounds at once, for they were the same ones that had haunted me since childhood. With a deep resignation, I made my way along the path, doomed to walk back and forth along the river for all eternity. I had become the very thing that I once most feared: I was a Shadow.

And his eyes have all the seeming of a demon's that is dreaming,
And the lamplight o'er him streaming throws his shadow on
the floor;
And my soul from out that shadow that lies floating on the floor
Shall be lifted—nevermore!

RESOURCES

Adams, Charles J. III. *Berks the Bizarre*. Reading, Pa.: Exeter House Books, 1995.

———. *Bucks County Ghost Stories*. Reading, Pa.: Exeter House Books, 1999.

———. *Coal Country Ghosts, Legends, and Lore*. Reading, Pa.: Exeter House Books, 2004.

———. *Ghost Stories of Chester County and the Brandywine Valley*. Reading, Pa.: Exeter House Books, 2001.

———. *Montgomery County Ghost Stories*. Reading, Pa.: Exeter House Books, 2000.

———. *Pennsylvania Dutch Country Ghosts, Legends and Lore*. Reading, Pa.: Exeter House Books, 1994.

———. *Philadelphia Ghost Stories*. Reading, Pa.: Exeter House Books, 2001.

Adams, Charles J. III, and David J. Seibold. *Ghost Stories of the Lehigh Valley*. Reading, Pa.: Exeter House Books, 1993.

———. *Pocono Ghosts, Legends and Lore, Book Two*. Reading, Pa.: Exeter House Books, 1995.

Asfar, Dan. *Ghost Stories of Pennsylvania*. Alberta, Canada: Ghost House Books, 2002.

Botkin, B. A., ed. *A Treasury of American Folklore*. New York: Crown, 1944.

———. *A Treasury of Railroad Folklore*. New York: Crown, 1953.

Brunvand, Jan Harold. *The Choking Doberman and Other Urban Legends*. New York: W. W. Norton, 1984.

———. *The Vanishing Hitchhiker*. New York: W. W. Norton, 1981.

Coffin, Tristram P., and Hennig Cohen, eds. *Folklore in America*. New York: Doubleday & AMP, 1966.

———. *Folklore from the Working Folk of America*. New York: Doubleday, 1973.

Cohen, David Steven. *The Folklore and Folklife of New Jersey*. New Brunswick, N.J.: Rutgers University Press, 1983.

Cohen, Daniel, and Susan Cohen. *Hauntings & Horrors*. New York: Dutton Children's Books, 2002.

Dorson, R. M. *America in Legend*. New York: Pantheon Books, 1973.

Editors of Life. *The Life Treasury of American Folklore*. New York: Time Inc., 1961.

Erdoes, Richard, and Alfonso Ortiz. *American Indian Myths and Legends*. New York: Pantheon Books, 1984.

Fiedel, Dorothy Burtz. *Haunted Lancaster County Pennsylvania*. Ephrata, Pa.: Science Press, 1994.

———. *Fiedel's Official Ghost Guide to Lancaster County Pennsylvania*. Lancaster, Pa.: Fisher Productions, 2002

———. *True Ghost Stores of Lancaster County, Pennsylvania*. Ephrata, Pa.: Science Press, 1995.

Flanagan, J. T., and A. P. Hudson. *The American Folk Reader*. New York: A. S. Barnes & Co., 1958.

Korson, George, ed. *Pennsylvania Songs and Legends*. Philadelphia: University of Pennsylvania Press, 1949.

Leach, M. *The Rainbow Book of American Folk Tales and Legends*. New York: The World Publishing Co., 1958.

Leeming, David, and Jake Page. *Myths, Legends, & Folktales of America*. New York: Oxford University Press, 1999.

Library of Congress Archive of Folk Culture. Songs and Ballads of the Anthracite Miner [compact disc]. Washington, D.C.: Library of Congress, 2000. Available at Hyperlink www.loc.gov/shop/index.php?action=cCatalog.showItem& cid=13&scid=70&iid=848.

McDowell, John. "The life of a coal miner." *The World's Work Magazine* (October 1902): 2659–60. Available at Hyperlink http://history.osu.edu/projects/coal/LifeOfCoal Miner/.

Peck, Catherine, ed. *A Treasury of North American Folk Tales*. New York: W. W. Norton, 1998.

Pierce, Arthur D. *Iron in the Pines*. New Brunswick, N.J.: Rutgers University Press, 1957.

Pitkin, David J. *Ghosts of the Northeast*. New York: Aurora Publications, 2002.

Poe, Edgar Allan. *Complete Stories and Poems of Edgar Allan Poe*. New York: Doubleday Books, 1966.

Polley, J., ed. *American Folklore and Legend*. New York: Reader's Digest Association, 1978.

Reeser, Tim. *Ghost Stories of Lancaster, PA*. Monocacy, Pa.: 1stSight Press, 2003.

Reevy, Tony. *Ghost Train!* Lynchburg, Va.: TLC Publishing, 1998.

Schwartz, Alvin. *Scary Stories to Tell in the Dark.* New York: Harper Collins, 1981.

Seibold, David J., and Charles J. Adams III. *Pocono Ghosts, Legends and Lore, Book One.* Reading, Pa.: Exeter House Books, 1991.

Skinner, Charles M. *American Myths and Legends, Vol. 1.* Philadelphia: J. B. Lippincott, 1903.

———. *Myths and Legends of Our Own Land, Vol. 2.* Philadelphia: J. B. Lippincott, 1896.

Spence, Lewis. *North American Indians: Myths and Legends Series.* London: Bracken Books, 1985.

Trapani, Beth E., and Charles J. Adams III. *Ghost Stories of Pittsburgh and Allegheny County.* Reading, Pa.: Exeter House Books, 1994.

Wilson, Patty A. *The Pennsylvania Ghost Guide, Vol. 1.* Waterfall, Pa.: Piney Creek Press, 2000.

———. *The Pennsylvania Ghost Guide, Vol. 2.* Waterfall, Pa.: Piney Creek Press, 2001.

Wincik, Stephanie. *Ghosts of Erie County.* Self-published, 2002.

Zeitlin, Steven J., Amy J. Kotkin, and Holly Cutting Baker. *A Celebration of American Family Folklore.* New York: Pantheon Books, 1982.

About the Author

S. E. Schlosser has been telling stories since she was a child, when games of "let's pretend" quickly built themselves into full-length tales acted out with friends. A graduate of Houghton College, the Institute of Children's Literature, and Rutgers University, she created and maintains the award-winning Web site Americanfolklore.net, where she shares a wealth of stories from all fifty states, some dating back to the origins of America. Sandy spends much of her time answering questions from visitors to the site. Many of her favorite e-mails come from other folklorists who delight in practicing the old tradition of who can tell the tallest tale.